DIRTY HANDS

Dirty Hands

DAVID HALL
with contributions by
IAN COFFEY, DAVE POPE &
DOUG BARNETT

KINGSWAY PUBLICATIONS
EASTBOURNE

ISBN 0 86065 476 1 (Kingsway)
ISBN 1 85078 020 X (STL)

Biblical quotations are from the
New International Version, © New York International
Bible Society 1978.

Front cover design by Phil Thomson

STL Books are published by Send the Light
(Operation Mobilisation), P.O. Box 48, Bromley,
Kent, England.

Printed in Great Britain for
KINGSWAY PUBLICATIONS LTD
Lottbridge Drove, Eastbourne, E. Sussex BN23 6NT by
Richard Clay (The Chaucer Press) Ltd, Bungay, Suffolk.
Typeset by CST, Eastbourne, E. Sussex.

Contents

Foreword *by* Cliff Richard   7
Introduction   9

PART ONE

1. Clean Hearts and Dirty Hands   13
   by Ian Coffey

PART TWO

2. John Goodfellow—A Journey from Fraud to
   Freedom   33
3. Anne Townsend—Challenges Unlimited   52
4. Pradip Sudra—From the Banks of the Ganges
   to the Backstreets of Britain   72
5. Hilary Smith—The Copper Who Learned to Cry   88
6. Paul Shepherd—One of God's Eastenders   108
7. Ken Gnanakan—A Vision for India in a
   Council House in Ruislip   129
8. Jim Gilchrist—Peacemaker on the Streets   145
9. Jack Norwood—Engineering for the Kingdom   165
10. Dave Pope—Starting Where You Are   179

PART THREE

11. Where Do We Go From Here?
    by Doug Barnett   193
    Postscript   210

Foreword
by
Cliff Richard

The older I get as a Christian (and I've notched up a good few years by now!) the more I am aware that probably the most critical balance in any Christian life is the one between belief and action; of backing up our passionate words and precious doctrines with obedient lives. 'Clean hearts and dirty hands' is how this book simply and neatly summarizes these two equally vital components of Christianity and, with hindsight, it may have been wise to have gummed a warning sticker to the cover—I have a gut feeling that there will be a whole lot of people making major lifestyle changes once they have read and digested what follows. Certainly you need to prepare for a challenge!

I guess it's common knowledge that Tear Fund was particularly instrumental in helping me remove the blinkers and look out on a world that needed food, dignity, and the good news about a God who loves. Visits with Tear Fund directors to countries such as Bangladesh and India, Sudan and Haiti, have caused poverty and starvation statistics to take on flesh and blood. And, believe me, watching it all on the TV screen at home is no substitute. When you see and smell and touch for yourself, you're never quite the same again. I am well aware that my hands are not nearly as grubby as they could be or should be, but at least they're a little less lily-white than before.

As you read the following exploits of a group of remarkable and courageous Christians, there is a danger of assuming that in some way they are special people—a different super-spiritual breed, who know nothing of domestic responsibilities or personal fears, and who are immune to the barrage of doubts, insecurities and temptations that cause us to trip and stumble so often. Not so! There's no such animal as a graduate in Christianity. We're all learners, all vulnerable, and all subject to similar problems and tensions. But the flip side of the coin is that we can all patch into the same power and the same grace, and grab hold of the truth that whoever God calls he also equips.

Good reading, and fruitful hand-soiling!

CLIFF RICHARD

Introduction

This book is a team effort. It had a unique beginning and a unique development.

The desire that lies behind it is to show, through the lives of nine men and women, how God can take and use ordinary people to make a difference in his world.

Ian Coffey has written the opening chapter detailing the beginnings of the Dirty Hands project and setting the whole message of this book into context.

David Hall is responsible for the bulk of the book. From hours of personal interviews—some of them conducted abroad—and through letters, phone calls and reading published articles, he has drawn together the stories of eight men and women who have answered God's call.

Dave Pope contributes an autobiographical note with an account of his own experience in responding to God's call to Christian service.

Doug Barnett writes the final chapter which looks at the ways in which we can discover God's will for our lives.

The four contributing writers wish to place on record their gratitude to the Dirty Hands Project Executive Committee, under the chairmanship of David Gray, as well as to Steve Chilcraft the Project Administrator.

Special thanks are due to those who have allowed their stories to be told—sometimes with great frankness.

This book is dedicated to the thousands of Christian men and women who are, right now, getting their hands dirty for God.

PART ONE

I

Clean Hearts and Dirty Hands

by

IAN COFFEY

We mounted the steps to board the giant airbus. We strapped ourselves into the seats and began to enjoy the cooling effect of the cabin's air-conditioning system— which provided some relief from the sticky night air outside on the tarmac. My friend and colleague, Dave Pope, and I were in the middle of our first visit to the vast subcontinent of India. We settled ourselves down for the long flight to New Delhi, the country's capital city.

The impact of that first visit to India has left a deep impression on both our lives, and the effect has never left us. During the course of that long flight we began to talk about the sights, sounds and smells of a country so very different from the one in which we had both been brought up. Some of our experiences had been hilarious—and others profoundly moving. We had met with people of different races and religions, tasted some unforgettable meals and shared a few sleepless nights. But within the montage of memories were two outstanding features.

Firstly, there was the incredible *need* that bombarded our emotions. We had come face to face with examples of physical need, terrible examples that defy description. It is one thing to see the face of a starving child gazing at you

from the page of your morning tabloid, but quite another
to come face to face with a homeless nine-year-old beg-
ging in the rain on the streets of Bombay. It is easier to
turn the page and hurriedly occupy your mind with an
advert for Microwaves than it is to settle down in a warm
bed when, a few hundred yards away, whole families are
sleeping on the hard, cold street. And that need was not
only physical; we were struck too by the spiritual need in a
land which boasts so many religions. We had spoken to
hundreds of people in halls, schools and churches. Their
eagerness to hear simple Bible teaching was something we
had not encountered before anywhere in the world.

Secondly, we were struck by the *opportunities* that surrounded us on every side. At that time—in 1982—it was
not even necessary for a holder of a Commonwealth passport to apply for a visa to enter India. Today, English
remains the common, binding language in a country with a
multiplicity of languages, dialects and cultures. Christian
workers had told us of their visits to remote village communities where a simple sketchboard talk, a film or the
sale of Christian books was welcomed as an important
event in the social calendar. Crowds of people would
eagerly sit to listen and queue to buy books. Alongside
these stories were first-hand accounts of spiritual warfare.
We heard reports of hostile receptions and even physical
attacks, where mobs were manipulated by anti-Christian
forces.

Before boarding our plane for the internal flight we had
spent some time at a Christian Training Institute where
young men and women, in addition to being taught the
biblical principles of evangelism, were also learning how
to express the love of Jesus Christ in practical ways. They
were receiving training in primary medical care and were
learning how to teach villagers to improve their water supply system and implement new methods of agriculture, so
that the overall life of a community could be changed for

the better. (You can read more about the work of the ACTS Institute in Chapter 7 where Ken Gnanakan's story is told.) We had been hit—with no little force—by the needs and opportunities of India and with the challenge to get involved. These enormous needs and opportunities seemed to lie side by side for any willing enough to take them up. We were both challenged by the lives of dozens of ordinary Christians, many from Europe and North America, who were seeking to express their love and faith in Jesus Christ to the people of India. They had turned their backs on comfortable careers and secure surroundings in order to do something great for God. Not many of them would be seen on the platforms of the large Christian conventions in their home countries. Not many of them would have their sermons in print or their photographs emblazened across the Christian press. But in their own way, by the power of God's Spirit, they were seeking to emulate the life of servanthood as lived out by Jesus. They were getting their hands dirty for God.

The aircraft slowly tipped its wings in a change of course and our conversation turned to a subject which would ultimately serve to re-adjust the direction of the Team of which Dave and I were a part. We reflected on the tragic lack of world vision among so many Christians in Western Europe and North America. As we talked we began to realize that *we* were a part of that problem. All of us who are engaged in Christian leadership have a duty to point those who follow us to a world beyond our own local churches or organizations. That does not mean that serving God where we are is unimportant. But the biblical examples of leaders such as Paul, Peter, John—and supremely the example of the Lord Jesus Christ himself—reveal that we need constantly to be saying to those we are leading—'*You are involved in something far bigger than the things that you see with your own two eyes.*'

Open your eyes

Jesus in his parting words to the disciples told them that their task was to preach the gospel firstly to their fellow countrymen, then to those of a foreign culture who were their natural enemies and ultimately to the four corners of the earth.

As Christian leaders we must never forget that God's priority is Mission World. All too often we become caught up in planning our own programmes, servicing our own agendas and, sadly, at times building for our own self-interests. God calls us to be kingdom-builders not empire-builders. The familiar words of Jesus are often quoted from our pulpits: 'I tell you, open your eyes and look at the fields! They are ripe for harvest' (John 4:35). How often do we practise those five powerful little words, 'Open your eyes and look'? We sometimes sing, 'Open my eyes, Lord, I want to see Jesus.' That is a noble aspiration, for until we see him and understand something of his kingly majesty and authority, our service in his name will be shallow. But how often do we pray, 'Open my eyes, Lord, to see your world as you see it'?

I remember once speaking to a man at the end of an evening service. He asked an honest question about prayer. He told me that he found he was able to pray for his family, workmates and church but found it difficult to broaden his prayers beyond this narrow circle. 'How can I learn to pray for the world?' he asked me.

'Open your eyes,' was my answer. The news bulletins on television and the headlines in our daily papers give us more than enough fuel for prayer. We all need to learn to watch, to listen—and in Jesus' name, to pray and to act.

Clean heart—dirty hands

During the course of that long flight we sensed that God

was giving us a new direction, or more accurately a bigger vision. Part of that enlarged vision was the need to bring the challenge to Christians—'God wants *you* to have a clean heart—but dirty hands.'

As the months passed we began to work out the implications of something we believed God had given us as an idea, a dream, a burden and a vision; all those words wrap up what was becoming to us a clear direction from the Lord. We took time to consult and pray with other teams involved in ministries similar to the Saltmine Trust and we paid attention to their wise words of advice. In time something which became known as 'The Dirty Hands Project' came into being. Through a series of events held in different parts of the British Isles we sought to share something of our God-given burden that Christians of all ages and backgrounds need to take a step forward and become involved in the priority of Mission World.

It was during the many hours of preparation for the project that this book you are now reading came into being. We came to see that one of the best ways to 'earth' any challenge is to see it worked out in the everyday lives of people. We decided to draw together the stories of ordinary people who, right now, are attempting extraordinary things for God.

We faced a difficult task. How do you put across on paper the life stories of individuals and their varied experiences of God within the limitations of a few thousand words? As the saying goes, 'Things are better felt than telt.' Also we had the problem of deciding whose stories were the ones that should be told. We faced the danger of glamorizing ordinary men and women and making them into superstars or spiritual heroes—something which all of those included in this book steadfastly wanted us to avoid.

In the end, after a great deal of careful thought, we decided on the people whose stories you are about to read. They would be the first to acknowledge that they are a small group among many who are serving God around the world today. In one sense they are nothing special, except of course to God and those who love and care for them. But their lives are walking, talking illustrations of what God can do with those who are prepared to do something for this world and the next.

As I have read the manuscript which David Hall has skilfully put together from personal interviews, letters and articles, I have been challenged and helped to see how God is able to use anybody who is willing to take him at his word and move forward in faith.

A number of interesting common denominators emerge from the stories contained in this book. It is worth noting them as you read:

  *God chooses quite ordinary people to serve him.
  *Serving the Lord Jesus Christ effectively must flow from a life surrendered to him.
  *Hindrances, failures and weaknesses of background do not disqualify but qualify us for serving God.
  *Getting our hands dirty for God begins in the place where we are. Faithfulness in the small things leads to being entrusted with greater things.
  *Fear is something which by God's power we can face and overcome.
  *Faith and obedience are indispensable when we serve God.
  *Detours are not roadblocks to the outworking of God's purposes.
  *There is no greater fulfilment in life than doing God's will in the place where he has put you.
  *There is no limit to what God can accomplish when a man or woman is totally committed to doing what he tells them.

Starting school

My eldest son came out of school after his first day totally disillusioned. Enjoyment was not written across his five-year-old face. 'What's the matter?' we asked him anxiously. 'I've been there a whole day and I still can't read!' he replied.

For months he had been told, 'When you go to school you will learn to read.' In his childlike way he had expected it to happen just like that, all in a day.

We are all children at times, wanting instant results. But it is impossible to sow and reap in a day. Growth takes time and sustained growth takes longer. You are reading this book (I hope) because you want to! Possibly you are at a crossroads in your own life and are looking to God for directions. Let me warn you against the danger of expecting instant answers. God does on occasions give dramatic instructions about guidance. But more often than not it is the still small voice of the Spirit heard over a period of time and confirmed in different ways that reveals the next step.

Jesus told us to ask, seek and knock. That is what we must do, remembering that when God opens the door he usually brings us into the hallway for a time before gradually opening up the other rooms. The full-blown guided tour type of guidance appears to be the exception rather than the rule.

To change the direction of a ship you turn the wheel which controls the rudder. But in order to turn, the ship needs to be moving through the water. You cannot steer a stationary ship. In the same way, we need to be walking with God in our everyday lives and it is as we move on that he can steer us in his plan. That is why it is important that you develop in your relationship with Jesus Christ. The great missionary statesman J. Oswald Sanders once wrote, 'God does not force his intimacies on people. He grants them only to those who desire and qualify for them.'

Moses was one of God's inner circle. The Bible records, 'The Lord would speak to Moses face to face, as a man speaks with his friend' (Exodus 33:11). It is worth while discovering some of the lessons that Moses learned as God was calling him to his life-ministry.

Lessons for learning

Moses was eighty when he experienced a life-transforming encounter with God. The first forty years of his life were spent in an Egyptian palace where, by a series of divine interventions, he had been brought up and educated as a prince. The second forty years were spent as a runaway refugee working in the deserts of Midian with sheep as his principal companions. 'What a waste of a life,' he may have been tempted to say as he reflected on his chronicles of wasted time. But God never makes mistakes and never wastes the precious commodity of time. Every second of those long eighty years (and there were over twenty-five thousand million) was used by God to train him for the encounter at the burning bush which is detailed in Exodus chapter 3. That meeting with God led to forty years of vital leadership in the nation of Israel at the most crucial period of her history. God does not waste time. Compare Moses' eighty years of training for his forty years of service with the thirty years our Lord Jesus spent in obscurity and his three years of public ministry.

Too often we measure time by our own hour-glass, forgetting that God's is bigger.

God can even redeem wasted years and turn them around for his purposes. In that sense they become not a waste but an investment which he can take up and use.

Reading through Exodus chapter 3 we discover that God drew out five important lessons that he had been preparing Moses for throughout the years leading up to this encounter. Five lessons that we need to learn if our lives are going to count for God.

1. A lesson about himself

God spoke to Moses from a bush that burned yet was not consumed. As he went to examine this sight, strange even to a man used to the peculiarities of nature in the desert, God spoke and Moses responded. He was told to remove his sandals as this was a holy place and a holy moment. God spoke as the God who had appeared to Moses' forefathers, the great men of history, Abraham, Isaac and Jacob. God told him that he knew of the enforced slavery of his people Israel in Egypt. Moses could not forget them and God had not overlooked them. God intended to rescue them from their lives of bondage and to bring them into a good and spacious land of their own. He revealed to Moses his great rescue plan, which must have moved the refugee to the core of his being, and then God delivered the devastating message: 'So now, go. I am sending you to Pharaoh to bring my people the Israelites out of Egypt' (verse 10).

Moses paved the way for his first lesson about serving God with his understandable reply: 'Who am I, that I should go . . .?' (verse 11). It is a question that anyone asks when they first sense the call of God. For Moses it was loaded with a background of insecurity and fear.

You can understand his problem if you read the first two chapters of Exodus. He had quite a past to wrestle with:

    *He had been born at a time of crisis.
    *He was born in the most extreme conditions of uncertainty.
    *At three months he had been abandoned by a heartbroken mother.
    *He was taken home and cared for by his own family

but in the role of foster parents.
*At a tender age he was taken away and brought up in a palace in an alien culture.
*He lived a schizophrenic existence: inwardly a Hebrew and outwardly an Egyptian.
*He tried to do the right thing and ended up committing murder.
*He was rejected by his own people and had to flee for his life.
*He lived a refugee-life as a shepherd in another foreign culture.
*He married in exile and had a son. The boy's name reveals much of his father's heartache—*Gershom*: which conveyed the meaning 'an alien in a foreign land'.

Moses probably felt he had too much to sort out to be of any use to God. But how else could a leader be trained to take an entire nation through a wilderness for forty years? For the man who was going to be a leader in spiritual life, politics, military warfare and at the same time lay down a foundation for the coming kingdom of God, four decades as a prince in a palace followed by the same period as a shepherd in the desert were simply perfect preparation. So often the things that would seem to be disqualifications turn out, in God's economy, to be the ideal qualifications.

God's answer to Moses was short: 'I will be with you . . .' (verse 12).

The lesson is clear. It is not our ability, or our lack of it, that makes the difference—but God. It is not even great faith that counts, but what we put our faith in. The lesson for Moses is a lesson for us: with God nothing is impossible.

2. A lesson about God

Moses' second lesson again sprang from a question. It can be summarized in three words. He asked God: 'Who are you?' (see verse 13). Who was doing the sending for this seemingly impossible task? God's reply was infuriatingly brief yet utterly profound: '*I am who I am*' (verse 14).

This is a significant moment in the Bible. The God of Israel, the God and Father of our Lord Jesus Christ, is known as Yahweh (or Jehovah) which derives from this title '*I am that I am*'. But what God is saying is more important than just a title, the phrase tells us about his character.

Another way of translating it would be to say '*I will be what I will be*'. God was telling Moses something about his own unique, holy and glorious nature. He is the God who was and is, and is to come. God never stands still. He is not a lifeless carving or statue, but the dynamic active God of creation and history. Moses was learning the lesson that would keep him going through forty years of coping with a rebellious nation. God was teaching something about himself and his total ability to meet every situation which Moses would face. God wanted Moses to be sure of himself and sure of his God. So when people challenged him: 'Who do you think you are?' he could respond, 'I am what I am by the grace of God.' And when he was asked by whose authority he operated, the answer was apparent: '*I am.*'

Throughout his leadership years Moses knew himself and his God. The ground was marked out:

I am what I am—by the grace of God.

He is what he is—I am.

Know yourself and know your God—these are the first two lessons we must learn and apply for ourselves. In an insecure world we need firm foundations. God has revealed himself to us through his world, by his word and supremely in his Son, Jesus. He reveals his truth to us by the Holy Spirit who speaks through the pages of the God-breathed Scriptures as well as through godly Christian leaders and friends, his inner witness and the circumstances of life. We must know him before we attempt to serve him.

3. A lesson about the authority of God

The account of Moses' meeting with God continues into chapter 4. Again we find Moses asking difficult questions. 'What about them?' he says (verse 1). He poses the question with his mind on the people he is meant to lead who have rejected him. Moses seems to have had greater fears about God's people than Pharaoh's army—a situation which we all find ourselves in from time to time!

The heart of the matter was the issue of authority. What right did Moses have to assume this role? How could he stand against the obvious criticisms that would come?

In verses 2-9 we read that God gave him three signs to teach one lesson: the staff becoming a snake, the hand becoming leprous and the water becoming blood were fairly high on the Richter Scale of signs and wonders. But beyond the tokens lay a trust—*Omnipotence knows no limitations*.

Moses' authority lay not in himself, his qualifications or even his office—but in his God. When God calls someone to do a task he always gives them the right equipment. The problems arise when we reject the discipline of training and the development of skills. After all, we are told that Moses was 'no ordinary child . . . [he] was educated in all the wisdom of the Egyptians and was powerful in speech and action' (Acts 7: 20, 22). How could he be God's spokesman to Pharaoh if he had not spent tortuous hours wrestling with the nuances of Egyptian grammar as a teenager?

Moses learned the lesson, and then applied it through the difficult years that lay ahead. His authority was not man-made but God-given. Much lies behind God's question: 'What is that in your hand?' (verse 2). Moses was called to give God what he was holding—in this instance the shepherd's staff which, when thrown down in obedience, became a snake. When he took it up again it became a staff once more, the same staff but different. He never held it in the same way again. It became a token, a symbol that his authority for leadership was supernatural in every sense.

God faces us with the same question: 'What is that in your hand?' As we lay before him our gifts he allows us to take them up again, but they never feel the same. Too often service for God is seen in the light of natural skills fashioned by natural means, but this is simply not good enough. To serve effectively we must first learn the lesson of the true nature of spiritual authority.

4. A lesson about serving God

We can all identify with Moses' protest as the call of God became stronger: 'O Lord, I have never been eloquent, neither in the past nor since you have spoken to your servant. I am slow of speech and of tongue' (verse 10). His cry is echoed by all who sense God calling them to serve— 'I can't do it!' Moses was focusing on his lack of ability for the job he was being asked to undertake. Some scholars believe that he may have been referring to a speech impediment which could have been an after-effect of his traumatic early years.

Whether he was making an excuse or pleading a genuine case we cannot tell, but God's response was emphatic: 'Who gave man his mouth? Who makes him deaf or mute? Who gives him sight or makes him blind? Is it not I, the Lord? Now go; I will help you speak and will teach you what to say' (verses 11-12).

Resist the temptation to focus on the jar of clay or you will forget the treasure it contains. 'Christ in you, the hope of glory' is the mysterious truth of this gospel we have been called to believe and practise. (See Colossians 1:27.)

The issue for Moses—and for you and me—is whether

we are prepared to let God have all there is of us. If we are, we begin to make the wonderful discovery that, when we give God all there is of us, then all there is of him becomes available to us.

Perhaps, like Moses, you feel weighed down by personal inadequacies. Then you need to learn that effective service begins with that admission of weakness followed through by laying hold of all that God has promised to us in Jesus Christ. The same Spirit who raised Jesus from the dead can pour his creative life force through every fibre of a being given over to him. That is not possibility thinking but a positive, daily act of faith.

5. A lesson about obedience to God

A story is told about a lady who always sat in the front pew in church. Whatever the subject of the sermon, she would accompany it with stage whispers and nods of approval, applying relevant bits of the message for those in the congregation she thought needed to hear it. The minister knew of this lady's own spiritual need and her steadfast refusal to receive God's word for herself. During a morning service exasperation got the better of the pastor. As he made a telling point which he felt she needed to hear, he leant across the pulpit and pointing his finger said, 'And Mrs So-and-So, this is for *you*!'

Moses experienced that sort of thunderbolt guidance as he wriggled under the hand of God. He revealed the deep objection of his will as the divine call moved too close for comfort: 'O Lord, please send someone else to do it' (verse 13). Here was the crux. With all the excuses gone, was he willing to be obedient to God?

We read that the Lord's anger burned against Moses. But then in his grace he gave him Aaron as a mouthpiece, spokesman and companion (verses 14-16). Perhaps, in some senses, it was God's second-best. But God's ability to meet a real human need must never be underestimated.

God recognized Moses' sense of vulnerability and gave him the human support that he needed—even if Aaron at times proved to be more of a problem than a solution.

We also wrestle with the issue of loneliness, and it is a heavy weight many carry in serving God. You may be single and find yourself, albeit subconsciously, laying down the pre-condition that you will serve God if he gives you a life-partner. He understands the cry of your heart, but are you willing to say yes to his will *unconditionally*? It is a hard-hitting challenge, but one we cannot walk away from if our lives are to be lived in the enjoyment of God's best.

So, enter Moses the reluctant hero, who gives so much hope to those of us who sense God's call and feel overwhelmed with doubts and questions. He moved forward in God's purpose for his life and discovered that obedience multiplies blessing. The history of nations was staked on his willingness to go God's way, and the ultimate ushering in of God's kingdom and its blessings for the world were wrapped up in that encounter in the lonely desert. God often begins his most enterprising schemes in unlikely places with unlikely people. The life of Moses stands as a landmark for all who want to live lives that are of worth for God. We would do well to learn from his lessons.

Out of the classroom

July 13th 1985 is a special day to be remembered. Billed as 'The greatest show on earth' Live Aid rocked the world. Through the vision, genius and sweat of a ranting rock star, millions were raised and thousands saved. The plight of the starving people of Ethiopia motivated Bob Geldof to get up and do something. Not for the first time God chose an unlikely instrument, I believe, to accomplish something important. I know nothing about Geldof's religious beliefs, but I do sense that, whether he was aware of it or not, he was used by God.

Writing of the event in retrospect the irate Irishman recorded:

'Please remember this day all of your lives. It's important.
Remember the day you wanted to help.
Remember the bands and the crews who did it. The professionals who made it an extraordinary technical feat.
Remember the dying who were allowed to live.
Remember on the day you die, there is someone alive in Africa because one day you watched a pop concert.
Remember your tears and your joy.
Remember the love.
Remember on that day for once in our bloody lives we won.
Remember that even though it's over, it need not stop.'

You may be puzzled that I should quote a secular entertainer and refer to the success of a secular event. But the point is vital. Because he cared, he did something.

Commitment is not something to which we as Christians can lay an exclusive claim. We see commitment exemplified in the Olympic athlete who, hours before most of us are out of bed, pounds the streets in a disciplined workout. You can find it in the university where a determined student turns down a stack of social opportunities because of a driving ambition to be the best. Commitment is seen in the young executive working all hours to gain promotion or in the face of a political activist pushing leaflets through doors in the pouring rain because he believes in a cause. Perhaps the difference between commitment in the church and commitment outside it is that as Christians we talk about it while others get on and demonstrate it.

If there's one word that summarizes the whole message of this book it is *involvement.* The challenge of the stories you are about to read is whether or not you are willing to get up and do something. We are not advocating mindless hyper-activism in the false belief that busyness equals effective service for God. But are you willing to listen out for God's voice as you read these pages? He wants you to face up squarely to the issue of involvement in his work in his world. It may mean leaving your job—on the other hand, it may mean going back to it with a fresh understanding of God's calling. Are you willing to get involved in the wonderful task of proclaiming the kingdom of God, pointing to it and in some sense actually representing it?

The response to the call to get involved may lie in one or more of these areas:

1. To commit yourself to pray regularly, intelligently and specifically for the unfinished task of world mission. This means becoming better informed about what is happening around the world, receiving regular prayer information and disciplining your own use of time.

2. To commit yourself to give financially, obediently and sacrificially to world mission.

3. To consider the possibility of short-term service for God.

4. To use a holiday, take early retirement or see redundancy as an opportunity to learn about serving God in a practical way.

5. To be open to God's call to you for an extended or even life-time commitment to Christian service—wherever that may be and whatever form that may take.

One thing is certain. You must begin where you are now. In front of you, all around you, lie opportunities to express the love of God in a hurt and dying world. It is no use dreaming about what you would do if you were a thousand miles away. Serving begins in your own backyard and step one for you may well be in your local church or community.

Are you willing to move out in faith for God—with a clean heart and dirty hands?

PART TWO

2

JOHN GOODFELLOW
A Journey from Fraud to Freedom

When twenty-six-year-old, long-haired hippy, John Goodfellow, and his three friends flung their rucksacks down in
the corner of a room in an Amsterdam hostel the name on
the board outside was the last thing on their minds. For
despite the title—Christian Youth Hostel—and the fact
that the quartet were in Holland to pull off a couple of
fraud deals so that they could earn enough cash to get to
Iran and hunt for a spiritual experience, they never once
considered looking to the Christian church for the answer
to their problems.

'It didn't occur to me,' said John. 'The church wasn't
interested in my problems. I wanted to get to Iran and
study the whirling dervish religious sect—they had some
answers, of that I was sure.'

Brought up a Roman Catholic, the confession-sin-confes-
sion-sin ritual had suddenly been rejected when he was
fifteen. 'I felt such a hypocrite,' was his youthful sum-
mary.

John's family were shocked by his rejection of the family faith. His father was a hard-drinking, hard-fighting
Irishman, the foreman of a gang of workers in the power

station construction industry, who was sent to work all over England. His mother, a nurse with a heart of gold, had plenty of questions about life herself.

John got a taste for alcohol early in life. By the time he was fourteen he would often turn up to school in Nottingham on Monday mornings with a hangover. At nineteen his bricklaying merely financed a heavier intake of drink. The funds to satisfy his thirst, however, could not be covered solely by his apprenticeship—so he turned to breaking into cars to get more money. But that was only the start. Eventually he needed more. One night, when his girlfriend left him, he snarled his way out of the discotheque, stole a bottle of whisky, and got drunk. As he wandered the streets of Nottingham in his drunken state he spotted a jeweller's window with a tempting array of valuables on display. He decided to try his hand at smash-and-grab. Helping himself to a road-side safety lamp that was guarding a building site, he smashed it through the window and dived inside. As he twisted round in the confines of the window he grabbed bracelets, rings and watches, stuffing them into his pockets and every conceivable space on his clothing. Then he snatched a couple of cards of bracelets and leapt from the window.

He had hardly begun to race down the street before sirens indicated the arrival of police cars—much earlier than the young thief thought possible. He flung himself into the labyrinth of passages around the town centre in an effort to escape. Sliding down steps he kept running, hiding for a few valuable seconds behind the protective wall of St Nicholas's Church. As he gasped for breath he heard another sound which made his blood run cold; the yapping of police dogs as they strained after him. It was quite a chase—one which John lost. Cornered by the baying dogs and the red-faced Nottingham policemen he was pinned against a wall. His arm was held behind his back and he was frog-marched to a car and taken to the police station.

Two days in the cells were followed by two months on bail awaiting trial. As a first offender John received a suspended sentence of two years—a small price to pay but enough to make him determined not to get caught again. Crime began to take over his life. He tried fraud—and earned himself several hundred pounds with a particularly ingenious scheme. Then, along with friends, he turned to mugging. Poised in the darkened alleyways of Nottingham's city centre they would pounce on likely suspects, drag them into the alley, beat them and grab what money happened to be available. For John, crime was beginning to get more brutal. Often he would beat someone near to death, and as his victim lay moaning on the road he would laugh his way into the nearest pub to spend the stolen money, his shoes and trousers sporting the blood-stained evidence of his brutality.

'I was becoming more violent, more angry, more rebellious. I was twenty years old but inside, was just like a kid of twelve—afraid, lonely, and angry with the world.'

His apprenticeship as a bricklayer completed, John decided to travel. The sun of Spain lured him and it proved easy to get work as a waiter and bouncer in a disco on the Costa Brava. 'I wasn't very big (just under six feet tall) but my father had taught me how to settle arguments with my fists. I was vicious and not afraid of anyone. I kept a home-made club behind the bar, but if that was unavailable would use a bottle or anything to sort out troublemakers.'

By now John wasn't existing simply on drink and violence; he had tasted drugs and was heavily into amphetamines. The little pills kept him going for two or three days at a stretch without sleep, wrecking his body. As his weight slumped to eight and a half stones from his previous eleven stones, he realized something had to be done. 'I knew I was killing myself. I desperately wanted to break the cycle of life that was ruining me,' he said.

When he was in Nottingham one winter he saw an advert asking for bricklayers in Canada. He landed in St John, New Brunswick, determined to control his life instead of allowing it to control him and vowing to give up drink, drugs and violence. 'I wanted a car, a wife, a house of my own and knew I would have none of those things if I carried on behaving the way I had been.' It was a vain hope.

For two tense months he fought to reduce his drinking and addiction. But a man in an apartment in the same house was his downfall; a drug pusher, he not only kept John liberally supplied but encouraged him to sell drugs. The rebirth of his love for drink and drugs beat him. Six months later, having been flung out of his rooms for non-payment of rent and reduced to working only occasionally when sober, he was living in a cheap, seamy room.

One day, lying on the rickety double bed that dominated the room, he stared at the ceiling. As if a video had been switched on he began to see his life flashing before his eyes. 'I had heard it happened when you died—but I wasn't dead.' As his life unfolded he realized he lacked the power to change himself. 'I knew I couldn't do anything for myself. For the first time I realized I had no power over my own life . . . Something snapped. I let out a silent scream of anguish.'

Something had died inside him. He saw himself at twenty-five ruined, an alcoholic, drug-addict, and on the run from everything and everyone.

'What's the matter with you, Johnny?' his friends asked when he returned to England. They could tell something was wrong. He couldn't handle life. But that experience in Canada launched John's quest for a new meaning in life. 'I suddenly needed to know what life was all about, who I was, what the point of life was, what I was doing on this planet . . . .'

An old friend showed him a thick book on the occult. Together they pored over it for hours, practising some of its sinister recommendations. He thought astrology might have the key, until a visit to leading astrologers in London put him off. 'They have nothing to offer. They're a bunch of idiots,' was his verdict.

'I asked if there was a God. Where was he? Could I contact him?' Even as he propped himself up on the bars of Nottingham's pubs, drunk and drugged, the questions poured from his stumbling lips until friends were tired of trying to answer and thought he was going crazy.

John decided the answer lay in Iran. His sister had spent six months with the mountain people, and he had been impressed by what he had read of the whirling dervishes. 'They had to have the answers. All I needed was money to go out there, buy a horse, travel with the nomadic tribes, smoke dope and hunt for God.'

The fraud that John had successfully pulled off some years before came back to his befuddled mind. He would try it again! Gathering three friends, they agreed the scheme; four times they would pull the fraud off—twice in Amsterdam, once in Belgium and once in France. With the money they would buy a mini-bus and drive to Iran.

So the foursome went to Holland, and signed in at the cheapest place they could find—the Christian Youth Hostel. If anything, the name of the establishment would provide a useful cover for their unlawful scheme. The Dutch frauds went according to plan; ten days after arriving in the capital they were ready to leave. Preparing to move on, they decided on a last night of merry-making before the next stage of their adventure. The night was for celebrating. A tattered notice on the wall of the hostel intrigued them: 'Free music on the Ark,' it offered. 'I thought we would go and get drunk and get some dope,' John said.

They made for the two battered-looking houseboats

jointly named the Ark, which were moored a couple of hundred yards from the station in the east docks. The 150 feet long boats looked the sort of dingy place which offered a lively evening. The four stepped on to the quayside where the two boats were tied up. Moving carefully on to the huge iron prow they edged along the foot wide ledge round the boat and peered into a window. Through the condensation they could see a small band playing on a raised platform at one end of the long room. Up to fifty people were sitting drinking. It looked good.

They manoeuvred round the thin walkway, carefully avoiding the narrow gaps between the boats as the two vessels rose and fell with the slight swell. Pushing open the wooden door they were greeted by a smiling Dutchman, who seemed unabashed by John's greasy blue suit, yellowy skin, and hacking cough from the drugs. Ignoring his greeting they ambled into the room and flung themselves on to some of the chairs dotting the walls. As they contemplated the scene they realized there was no alcohol—and certainly no drugs. An American girl smiled at them, introducing herself as Sherry, and launched into a conversation about Jesus. 'It was the first time anyone had talked about the gospel to me,' recalled John. 'It really embarrassed me. I had to get out.' So, panicking, John and his friends left for a real bar and drank themselves into oblivion.

Next morning they made for the Central Station and the bank of telephones. As they attempted to cram their four bodies into one of the small yellow-trimmed kiosks outside the station they were greeted by a voice. 'Hi there.' It was Sherry. She was late for work, having got almost to the office where she was working part-time, only to discover she had left her purse on the Ark. Returning to collect it, she recognized the four from the previous evening. She insisted they went for a coffee and again—even in the restaurant—the conversation revolved around Jesus and how Sherry had been born again.

When she invited them to the Ark that evening for a meal something impelled the four to accept—their time in Amsterdam was about to be extended. 'Somehow her obvious love and compassion was getting to us,' John admitted.

And it got to them even more that evening. Arriving at the Ark they discovered about thirty-five Christians and a dozen or so 'guests' like themselves sitting down for a meal. As they ate, the respect and concern the Christians had for them began to reach John. 'I couldn't understand it—no one had ever treated me like that before.' The first meal developed into a regular nightly visit until the four were invited to live on board the Ark. John and his friends grabbed their belongings and pitched below deck on one of the two boats, sleeping in a long dormitory with banks of double bunks round the walls, for themselves, and the dozen or so men also living on board.

In the afternoons they helped with practical work on the boats; in the evenings they began to enjoy the service of worship which followed the meal. Led by the towering long-haired figure of Floyd McClung, who had had the idea of the boat ministry a few years before, the foursome sat for long periods singing and listening to teaching from the Bible. On one occasion John heard other voices joining the singers. 'I realized it was a heavenly choir. It certainly wasn't anyone in the room. I heard voices over and above those on the boat.' That angelic choir broke him down. 'God's Holy Spirit came upon me and I just burst into tears, weeping uncontrollably for a quarter of an hour.'

The same thing was to happen on a number of other occasions during the five months John lived on the Ark. It was too much. One day he simply knelt alongside his bunk and asked Jesus to come into his heart and change his life. It was an amazing experience. John knew his heart had instantly been changed. He knew that the trip to Iran was unnecessary—on a houseboat in Holland he had met with God in a way that was going to revolutionize his life.

That conviction was reinforced days later as he was sitting in the boat's lounge talking to one of the workers about the return of Jesus. 'I didn't realize Jesus was coming back. It was a total mystery to me.' But as they talked he sensed Jesus standing right above him. 'He was big and had his arms wide open, round me. He spoke straight to my heart: "John, I love you, you belong to me now, I accept you. You are mine."'

Once again John was moved to tears. The Holy Spirit came upon him with wave after wave of love, like the gentle rocking of the boat as a larger vessel ploughed its way past in the harbour. From that moment the Bible became an open book. He began to read it feverishly, and to understand it. Words, phrases and passages leapt out at him with meaning. His friends recognized the change and were staggered. 'They just couldn't understand what had happened to me. I stopped cursing; didn't need to get drunk or take Speed or even smoke. I just didn't want those things any more. No one had told me to stop—the moment I met with Jesus I was set free in a most remarkable way.'

For two and a half months he enjoyed life on the boat, immersed in the Bible and discovering more about God. Another of his friends became a Christian and together they were baptized in one of Amsterdam's churches. But something was niggling in the back of John's mind. It was to do with his reason for being in Holland: he had gone, not to be changed, but to use the country as a base for fraud. 'I knew deep down that I had to do something about it. I couldn't be a Christian and live with the knowledge of what I had done.' He also knew that the police were looking for him in England in connection with the frauds. They had been alerted by the Christian manager of an insurance company who had felt uneasy about paying out on one of the claims. The manager had contacted the police who discovered other claims and pieced together the elements of the fraud system. John was wanted for conspiracy to fraud—a serious charge with severe penalties.

John telephoned the police in Nottingham. 'I want to give myself up,' he told the station officer. 'I'm John Goodfellow and you want me for fraud. I'm living in Amsterdam.' The police officer could hardly believe what he was hearing. John indicated on which boat he would be arriving in England and booked an appointment to meet the police at Harwich docks.

As the ferry struggled across the North Sea for eight hours John tried to remain calm, imagining what God wanted to do with him. Would it be witnessing in prison? The boat docked and shouldering his duffle-bag, John followed the noisy holidaymakers along the winding stairs and down the gangplank, accompanied by a couple of friends from the Ark who had made the journey to offer help. He joined the queue waiting at the passport desk and noticed two men, obviously plain clothes detectives, waiting alongside the uniformed customs officer. They moved towards him as he was tucking his passport back into the pocket of his jeans. 'Mr Goodfellow? Please come with us.'

John was led to a black police van and driven to the police station at Harwich. After writing down his statement, signing it, and being charged he was allowed to go free. John and his two friends were overjoyed and thanked God. 'I'm sure it was only because I had given myself up. They were very friendly—in fact they seemed puzzled.' John had grabbed the opportunity to explain why he had given himself up. 'It's because I have become a Christian,' he said, launching into his testimony.

This direct approach was to mark his spiritual life. The

trial was scheduled for five months later—a busy five
months, John totted up all the companies, shops, discos,
clothing stores, banks and individuals he had cheated or
stolen from. The amount reached staggering proportions
but he knew there was only one thing he could do—he had
to repay the money.

He walked into the jewellery shop where his first venture into big-time crime had begun with the smash and
grab raid. 'I would like to see the manager,' he said. When
the young, smartly dressed, manager appeared John
cleared his throat and began. He explained about the theft
and said he wanted to ask for forgiveness. As he gave his
reason—'I have become a Christian'—the manager's
mouth dropped open.

John was to get the same reaction many times as he
made personal calls to confess his crimes and offer to repay. Sometimes the answer was, 'We don't want your
money but wish you well in your new life.' On other occasions it was a brisk, 'When can you start paying?'

John was aware that he couldn't possibly return all the
money at once so he committed himself to working hard
and repaying it over the following five years—according to
how his court appearance went. He began working as a
bricklayer, long tough hours. Each Friday he would consult the little blue book in which he kept a record of his
debts, go to the Post Office, and buy a string of Postal
Orders and send them off. Then he would give his mother
£15 for his keep and retain just £5 for his own personal
expenses during the week. It was a spartan existence but
all he could do to honour the people he had wronged. 'I
knew that whatever ministry I was to have couldn't be
blessed unless I made an effort at restitution.'

By the time the trial started, three of the four men
involved were Christians—the third being led to Christ by
John during a cross-country lorry drive. The fourth man
never did become a believer.

In the Crown Court John waited tensely for the verdict. He was given a two years' suspended sentence, and the four were told to repay the money. John's debts were now in the thousands—even though the money that needed repaying for the insurance frauds was shared between the four of them. Tailors, insurance companies, discos from which he had stolen money from the till—it was a seemingly endless roll of dishonour.

But the postal orders continued to leave his home each Friday. For two and a half years he slogged away building and paying, using his spare time to practise the evangelism that had introduced him to Jesus. His new faith tumbled off his lips at work and at home. When he returned from Amsterdam his family were amazed at his Christian witness. Inside a year all the members of the family living at home had become Christians. First his mother, and unmarried sister, who had a six-month-old baby son, and then his father, six months before he died. But John was not satisfied with that; he took his Bible onto the streets of the city.

The large market place and shopping precinct in the centre of Nottingham became his pulpit, with a growing band of Christians willing to stand with him, singing joyful songs and listening as he preached his heart out. His faith might be new, but it was a bubbling, sparkling dynamite that exploded in actions and words. His days on the streets of Nottingham were laying the foundation for a life's work with Youth with a Mission—the organization that was in charge of the Ark and the work in Amsterdam.

As John's street preaching began to draw crowds—and produce more Christian support—John realized he needed help and direction. His own church, now suddenly without a pastor, were not keen to help in the open-air so he appealed to YWAM. Floyd McClung the Director sent his best workers—a married couple, Paul and Mary Miller. They took charge of the work and John was appointed assistant, learning from the scholarly, mature Christians.

And he grabbed other opportunities. John was beginning to hear God's voice and understand it. It was a bit mystifying on occasions—like the time he was clearly told to give up his lucrative work as a bricklayer and work for a laundry. Without really knowing why, John obeyed. On the second day at his new job he was sent to help a driver, 'What do you like doing?' the driver quizzed.

John told him: 'I'm a Christian.'

The stunned driver considered for a minute and then fired another question: 'So you don't drink, smoke or have fun?'

John put him right on the fun score!

The driver then confessed that two weeks before he had seen a vision—a man stood before him with a black book labelled Bible. The man had told him, 'Read this book.' That same afternoon John bought a black Bible and gave it to the driver.

The following Monday John was back on his building site, feeling that the one new Christian was the reason for the switch. 'I was convinced God had used me in the way he wanted to during that week in the laundry.'

The fiery young outdoor preacher found it thrilling to share the gospel—he couldn't stop. With the growing realization that the streets of the world were to be his parish, he took his next step of faith. Just two and a half years after making his decision to repay all his debtors in full he felt God telling him to sign on for a YWAM course in Holland. 'I knew that this was to be a new element in my life, God wanted me to be a missionary. But I kept thinking about all the money I still owed. I realized that if I went to Holland I would not be earning—how could I repay the debts and keep my promise?'

Other mature Christians confirmed what he felt God was saying: Holland it was to be. John packed his bags and went to Heidebeek—a beautiful twenty-four acre farm in one of the most picturesque parts of Holland. Surrounded by forest it was a place of tranquillity—but could someone settle there who had a little blue book full of debts?

He could. During the next few years God was to honour John's commitment and, although the young preacher didn't earn any money, gifts always arrived in time to make the regular payments. It was one of John's most exciting moments when he licked the envelope and sealed his final payment to an insurance company to clear the last debt. Jesus Christ had already forgiven his greatest debt: now God had honoured his own commitment to those personal debts which enabled him to be finally freed from the past.

At Heidebeek John was flung into intense study and activity. He revelled in it. Some of the best speakers in the world arrived at the YWAM base to teach on a variety of subjects. He lapped it all up. When he started life on the base he was twenty-nine—a Christian for three years, yet with a faith that was being rapidly hardened and shaped by practical use and the determination he had to obey God. For three months he studied, followed by another three months of practical outreach work, witnessing and ministering to others. Then he was invited to be personally involved in leading five similar courses—helping to organize and give training. It was a rapid promotion.

The beautiful farmland setting was tailor-made for the man from the English Midlands. Ten white stone buildings surrounded a larger farm house, with the forest beckoning beyond. Rising at five o'clock each morning, John would escape into the woods, to wander beneath the trees or sit on a log and talk to God. He said, 'I wanted to be certain of my future. I wanted to be effective for God but knew that I had to be sure of what God wanted me to do.' Gradually it became clear that he was called to be an evangelist: but his audiences would not be gathered in a huge stadium or indoor arena. They would stand on the street corners and markets of major cities.

As he began to see the way ahead, another development was taking place: he met Terry, an attractive girl from South Carolina in America, who was a student at one of the courses. It wasn't just her beauty or her slim attractive figure that charmed John but her godly spirit. Their friendship developed—surprising, perhaps, since Terry was from a well-to-do middle-class American family and John, still sporting the long hair of a hippy, was a one-time drunkard, drug-addict and criminal.

The friendship grew and on a beautiful autumn day, with a chill wind adding its own blessing, they were married. The simple ceremony led by Floyd took place on a carpet of golden autumn leaves in the garden of the farm at Heidebeek. The previous summer John had fulfilled a growing desire—he had led a team of seventeen on the first YWAM Summer of Outreach. The team camped on a central camp site in Amsterdam and befriended youngsters on the site while also launching an aggressive programme of evangelism on the streets of the Dutch city.

Floyd had started the YWAM work in Holland in 1973 using the Ark for a quiet, yet dynamic work in keeping with his own gentle nature. It was long-term evangelism. John was brasher, more direct, and anxious to take the initiative, going directly to people in need of the good news. The year following their wedding, Terry and John spent twelve months in America, getting to know each other as husband and wife while John studied at a South Carolina Bible School. Richer in Bible knowledge, he returned in 1981 to rejoin the work in Amsterdam. While he had been away, YWAM had added to their premises in the city. The two boats—the Ark—were now overshadowed by a huge, five-storey, forty-seven room, broken-down building in the heart of the city centre, overlooking the Central Railway Station. All the advice they had received had urged them not to buy. The building, once the headquarters of the Salvation Army in Holland, had been sold to a speculator who had allowed it to deteriorate. But YWAM began to refurbish it, creating a coffee bar, bookshop and a communication centre which was to be the nerve-centre of their work in the city. It was to be called: the Samaritan's Inn.

John and Terry lived for two years in a small, dilapidated room at the top of the building, without a shower or sink. Somehow they eked out an existence in primitive conditions on £60 a month. All the while John was keen to revive his Summer of Service. His appetite had been whetted as he stood in Dam Square and gave his testimony to a growing army of listeners. People seemed to want to stop and listen to the earnest young Englishman. There was something infectious about the love and excitement he showed. But he had to wait a year, for while work was going ahead on the Samaritan's Inn another building was bought—this time in the centre of the city's Red Light area. The four-storey, twenty-room building was squashed between a satanist church and a hotel for homosexuals. Prostitutes blandly stared from the windows of neighbouring properties offering their services. Drug pushers hung about the small streets, but all this made it an ideal site for the Cleft, as it was to be called.

John helped with the purchase and then found himself in charge of the rebuilding squad. The building had previously been a cheap hotel used mainly by drug addicts— broken needles dotted around the floor told their own sad tale. In the kitchen, rotting food still lay on the plates, left behind when the decision to close the hotel had been made some years before. They gutted the building and created a neat, if spartan, coffee bar in the front of the building. The stone steps from the street—just a few yards from one of the city's hundred canals—led up into a lounge area dominated by a welcoming fireplace. A bar was built at the far end, leading into the kitchens.

As its name implied, the Cleft was to become a refuge in an area of wickedness and arrogant sin. It was a crucial work, part of a growing mission for YWAM in one of Europe's key cities.

The following year John managed to lead his Summer of Service again—with eighty youngsters making for the central campsite and using it as a base for the summer. Their patch of tents became a focus of hope on a site which was noted for its use by drug addicts and the tougher elements of the city. By the following year, 1983, a hundred youngsters were on the site, and another hundred based in the city. It was the final year John was to use tents for the living accommodation. For the blossoming work of YWAM and increasing vision led Floyd and John to select yet another building and earmark it for God's use. This time it was the enormous two-hundred-room, four-storey, former sailors' lodging house in the heart of the docks, right opposite the historic shipping museum, once the Naval headquarters. The huge building surrounded its own central paved area—a complex to test the spiritual imagination of any organization. Priced at more than 2.1 million guilders it was an enormous challenge—but one to which YWAM rose.

De Poort became their new centre for training and evangelism, a bustling, living testimony to the faith which changed John's life. And it meant that YWAM had accommodation for hundreds.

In 1984 300 young people arrived to spend the summer preaching and reaching people in the city. This turned out to be merely a prelude to the following summer, when the invasion reached 500.

They carried a coffin through the canal-side streets in a gigantic solemn funeral procession, pausing occasionally for the body to leap from inside the coffin and tell the watching, and surprised, audience that there was death in the city but Jesus was offering them life. Gospel music, a marching band and street drama electrified the holiday-makers and city workers that summer. And five different teams of up to a dozen young people each carried huge wooden crosses around the streets, stopping at strategic locations to tell the curious onlookers what it represented.

John's vision for reaching the city was taking off and it was doing so just a couple of years after one of Holland's leading newspapers had highlighted the growing army of false cults and sects operating in Amsterdam, naming YWAM as one! John grinned as he recalled it, reflecting that currently most of the cults are no longer to be seen in the city. The Christians, however, continue giving out the good news. Few of Amsterdam's 750,000 residents or 3 million summer visitors could have missed some aspect of the witness.

For John and Terry life is full. They now have their three-year-old Sandy to consider and John makes sure that there is family time, however busy his schedule. Work in Amsterdam is never done. In his small office on the ground floor of De Poort John prays, and plans more city invasions—and extends his faith to other parts of the world.

The Ark is the base for work among the city punks, with flourescent-haired, spikey topped Christians adding their own colourful personalities to the witness teams. This, despite the fact that one of the old houseboats is doomed—no one can now stop the growing leaks!

The Samaritan's Inn attracts a growing number to its coffee bar and bookshop, with many finding Christ; it is also the vital centre of the YWAM web throughout the city.

The Cleft, still precariously poised between satanic elements, continues to fight evil. One prostitute to whom Terry had been witnessing for a couple of months flatly rejected any thoughts of God. After Terry returned from America and was sitting in the Cleft drinking coffee one afternoon she was astonished when the woman bounded inside, hugged her with delight and proclaimed, 'I became a Christian two weeks ago.'

De Poort houses an increasing number of students, arriving to discover how to witness in tough, battleground situations and YWAM leaders from different countries on special management courses so that they can run Christian front-line enterprises in their own lands. Mission teams leave for all over the world—India, Greece, Italy, America—anywhere John senses that the trio of orange vans parked outside, and their load of volunteers, are needed.

Children's meetings are run from a basement room under the Cleft; a small but faithful group reach Moroccan and Turkish people in Amsterdam; and teenagers meet at De Poort.

If he ever has cause to wonder whether all the activity he is now involved in is worth while John doesn't have to think for long. Five years ago he spotted a couple of Scottish girls in the city—both eighteen—drinking heavily and living it up at the discos. He spoke to them and took them to the Ark. That same evening one became a Christian. Two weeks ago John had a card from her—asking for prayer as she had finished Bible College training and was going to be a missionary in Belgium.

A lad of sixteen was discovered selling his own body in prostitution because of a broken, depressed conscience. In the middle of the Red Light district he gave his heart to Jesus Christ. Now he is living with Christians in the country, starting a new life.

Mission workers have had personal threats: 'The work should be closed . . . .' 'You are going to die . . . .' 'The office will be smashed . . . .' And, worse still, murderous threats to their children.

There is no way that they will leave Amsterdam. 'This is God's city and we shan't rest until we have won it for him,' said John. Dressed in dark trousers, a woolley sweater under his heavy coat, he trudged through the snow on a bleak February Saturday. 'They're peddling drugs,' he murmured, pointing to a group of coloured youths. Then, 'She's fifty and still a prostitute,' nodding towards a window from which peered a gaunt, heavily made up, elderly face. As he walks he plans for more evangelism—another summer when Amsterdam will feel the might of the gospel. For John Goodfellow—one-time criminal, drunkard, drug-addict and lover of violence—life is lived with a sharper edge than ever. Despite the growing call for administration in his office at De Poort, he refuses to leave the streets of the city he has come to love, or to stop shouting from the street corners the message that changed his life.

He turned up a narrow street, away from the great Singel canal, and called to an elderly tramp. Slipping money into the hand of the bedraggled old man he spoke a few short words in the Dutch language he is mastering, and prayed an inward prayer. So far the tramp hasn't become a Christian. It can't be long!

3

ANNE TOWNSEND
Challenges Unlimited

The small mug is one of my memories. Painted on its side is a little boy trying to rescue plants falling off a cart—and underneath is printed my name. It was a gift from Anne Townsend. Not so much a present, actually, as a peace offering. It crossed in transit with a bunch of flowers I was sending her. They followed a difference of opinion when we worked together to produce Family magazine.

Anne is like that. Direct and honest—and with a heart as soft as gentle down. Her honesty has cost her more than a mug in the past; it has led her into trying situations. She was, for instance, among the first to write exactly what it was like on the mission field—and not what we all wanted to hear it was like. She's also faced extremes in job changes as God has continued to lead her along a pathway uniquely marked for someone of her talents.

Anne's first exposure to the realities of missionary sacrifice came early. It was two months before her father saw his new daughter after her birth in the Elizabeth Garrett Anderson Hospital, London, in 1938. He had to work out his notice as headmaster of an Indian boys' grammar school, in Madras, before returning from India.

Her parents had decided that their child was to be born

in England. They feared for her health if they were to remain in India—those were the days before antibiotics, and a high proportion of missionary children died overseas.

But the England they returned to was one preparing for war. Jobs were scarce and when Henry Cawthorne arrived home it was to work first in Devon as an inspector of schools and then in Upminster, Essex, for the local education authority. Eventually, when Anne was nine, the family settled in Stoke-on-Trent, where her father became deputy chief education officer. She still looks upon the West Midlands as her home. For fifteen years she was to love the Staffordshire countryside and trips to the big city of Birmingham. But above all, Anne loved learning, and was always thirsting for knowledge.

After two years at a local junior school she won a scholarship, as had her brother, Hugh, before her, and was sent to Queenswood boarding school in Hertfordshire, where she soon began to satisfy her thirst for education. Girl Guides also enraptured her and she eventually became a Queen's Guide. 'I remember going into the woods near the school and doing all kinds of impossible things, things I never thought girls could do! I hiked, camped, and learned basic car and cycle maintenance, electrics, carpentry as well as the usual girlish stuff such as cookery and how to bath a baby! On one occasion she and a small team were sent into the woods, each one carrying an orange, a box of matches and a raw egg. 'We had to cook the egg and eat it, I peeled the orange, being very careful to leave the skin in one piece, and then broke the egg into the skin and fried it over a small fire. It tasted revolting—but I won a prize.'

There was one drawback, Anne discovered, to being a scholarship winner at a public school. The uniform was grey with white blouses, purple ties with silver stripes, but while most of the members of the school choir wore purple gowns, scholarship children wore grey gowns. 'It was meant to be a badge of honour—it seemed more like a badge of shame,' recalled Anne. 'It made it so obvious that my parents couldn't afford to pay.' Anne didn't like to be different—it was years before she developed the individual streak that would enable her to help thousands.

Because she was such an energetic scholar her parents asked if Anne could be moved up a year, and the school authorities agreed. So the year before the equivalent of today's 'O' levels Anne lost all her school friends and found herself in a higher group. It was a traumatic move for another reason: the previous summer she had been sent by her parents to a Bible Churchman's Missionary Society youth camp—'They thought it would be good for me,' she said. 'I had no idea what I was going to.'

One evening the girls in Anne's dormitory were all going to a Youth for Christ rally so Anne tagged along. 'I understood for the first time that night why Jesus had died. When the chap who was speaking said that anyone wanting to accept Jesus Christ as Saviour should stand up I did so, immediately—to my total horror I found that only two of us were standing in the whole of Eastbourne Town Hall. I had never felt such a fool before.'

The next day during communion Anne prayed, 'Well, God, I don't know what happened to me last night but something did because I can sense that you are here with me now. Whatever it was, it was probably the most important thing that has ever happened to me. Because of it, I think you want to use my life to tell other people about it, so here I am—do anything you want with me from now on . . . .'

Those words were to precipitate Anne into an adventurous lifestyle that would involve her in several changes of direction. She began to read the Bible and joined the Girl Crusader Movement's postal Bible study scheme. A lady in Southern Ireland became her tutor, reading pages of questions and answers from her prolific pupil. In fact, so keen was Anne that the tutor eventually sent several lessons at a time to save postage and time.

Returning to school, and her new year, Anne discovered that the problem of being separated from her former friends was softened by the discovery of a new friend: Adrienne Nye, from a doctor's family in Beverley, Yorkshire. It was Anne's introduction to evangelical Christian family life. 'My family were Christians—but at that time I didn't think they were because they didn't speak the evangelical jargon I was picking up,' said Anne, whose mission in later life was to separate that same jargon from her own language.

Boarding school was followed at seventeen by university—straight into the second year of medical training at the Royal Free Hospital in London. In the university hostel, she was put into a room with Faith Rainer, 'A lovely Christian girl who taught me a lot,' Anne said. Faith eventually went to Addis Ababa as a university lecturer, where she was to die of hepatitis. It was her death that was to prompt Anne in later years to write her book *Prayer without Pretending*: 'Because I promised to pray for her—and didn't.'

After six months in the hostel Anne moved into the top floor of the grandiosely named Women's Farm and Garden Association near Bloomsbury Square. The Association let medical students rent flats in the top floor, so Anne had her own room and immediately set another pattern for her life. Her bed was tucked at one end of the long room, with a small book-case groaning with medical textbooks alongside it—*Gray's Anatomy* vying for space with her other most prized book, a large black Thompson's Chain Reference Bible. At the other end of the room was a small window, set high up the wall, under which was Anne's travel trunk, covered with a greenish travel rug which her parents had used in India. Plants added a splash of colour to the room and Anne created her own world with pictures, bedspread and cushions. For years these travelled with her transforming the rooms she lived in, making them intimate and welcoming.

She survived the cold of the winter months, not by feeding valuable shillings into the gas meter but by slipping into a sleeping bag to study—a habit which Anne has retained to this day for television viewing in the evenings! She loved studying—and there was plenty of it. In common with her fellow students Anne had one nasty moment. This happened when she was taken to the dissecting rooms and told, with a friend, to start work on the body which lay like plastic in front of her. 'The formalin preservative had a powerful smell which made us very ill for the first few days. I thought I would never make it, but eventually I got hardened to the smell and didn't even notice it.'

For all her love of studying her heart was partly elsewhere. One summer when she had been staying in Beverley with Adrienne they had been to a meeting conducted by a group of Christian medical students and at 'Swinemoor Sunset Sausage Sizzle' Anne met John Townsend. He had cut a dapper figure in his black blazer with the slanting black and white stripes of the emblem of St Bartholomew's Hospital where he was training.

'I was attracted by his openness, honesty, sincerity and integrity,' said Anne of the man who began to win her heart. John showed Anne round the various hospitals before she eventually began her training at the Royal Free, and because he was living at the Medical Missionary Association, near her own accommodation, they began to see a lot of each other. Christian girls in Anne's hostel and some of John's friends met regularly for fun runs through London late at night. One winter's run ended in Trafalgar Square where Anne decided to jump on to the ice in the fountains—only to discover it wasn't as thick as she had anticipated. 'The lads ran me all the way back to the hostel while my jeans crackled with the freezing water.'

John and Anne belonged to the South London Witness Team, regularly leading evangelistic services all over London. One summer they were invited to run the childrens work at a camp in Worthing. As they were strolling back to Anne's lodgings one afternoon, planning the meetings, John asked Anne: 'If, when you are twenty-one, I asked you to marry me, do you think you might say "yes"?' So they became engaged. The ring was bought in Birmingham. John had drawn out all his National Savings—£25, a lot of money in those post-war days. He had never had as much money in his life, so his mother stitched it carefully inside his trousers' pocket to keep it safe. It was an adequate safety precaution—but an embarrassment as they decided on a ring from the first shop they visited, and John had to stand in the corner casually unpicking his mother's neat stitches to get at his money. It was a gold ring with three diamonds—'To symbolize John and me with God in the middle,' Anne explained.

The couple were asked to be the overseas students' secretaries for the London Inter-Faculty Christian Union executive committee—the first engaged couple ever to be asked to have a job on the central committee together. It took a special dispensation from the IVF headquarters to allow it.

Two weeks after Anne qualified, they were married. Anne had a job at the Royal Free Hospital and John at Barts. But both jobs were 'on the house' and involved living in—in those days housemen, as both were, were not strictly 'supposed to be married' although it was impossible to prevent it. To further complicate matters, Anne had one night in three off and John alternate nights. So the inventive couple bought a blow-up mattress which was carried to the room of whoever was working that night. They carted this bed across London for six months until both got jobs together at Southend General Hospital. 'They were wonderful, they even converted two ground floor rooms into a nice flat for us,' Anne said.

Just a year and a quarter after Anne had qualified Janet was born.

For several years they had thought and prayed about a missionary society to contact. Anne was an Anglican and John a Methodist, but neither was concerned about denominational affiliations and they agreed to look at inter-denominational societies. Increasingly the Overseas Missionary Fellowship seemed to be the one most suited to them. Founded by Hudson Taylor in 1865, it was one with whose principles and practices Anne and John felt most at home. They began attending conferences run by OMF and got to know the candidates' secretary. They also became prayer partners of a couple of missionary doctors, so discovering more about the work that was soon to take sixteen years of their lives.

Six months after their wedding they applied to OMF. They were interviewed separately, John by two men and Anne by two women, before facing the candidates' committee—again separately. They were assessed first as individuals, and then as a couple. 'To our utter amazement, we were accepted. We never felt we could possibly be good enough. We felt OMF contained Christians of such calibre that we could never aspire to their heights. They all seemed to have so much faith and God did such wonderful things for them and through them . . . we were so ordinary by comparison.'

The training was long and hard. There was a candidate's course in which the OMF personnel got to know them— and they OMF. That included basic training in missionary principles, learning to live with other people, understanding OMF and how to 'live by faith'. After that came training at the former China Inland Mission headquarters in Newington Green, North London—they were given two rooms for themselves and Janet. Next they were sent to Merstham for three months, then the home of the Summer School of Linguistics, for basic language training. Three months' Bible study at Capernwray Hall completed the early stages of their missionary education.

Then came the day they sailed for Singapore—the OMF international headquarters and the place where they would discover just where God wanted them and in what capacity. John had worked extra duties as a locum—standing in for doctors on holiday and over weekends—to save their fares to Singapore, which was the only money they had to find. They left with a group of about twenty other candidates, and with hundreds of people lining the station platform at Victoria. The words of the hymn, 'God be with you till we meet again' echoed along the railway lines as they left London behind, bound for an even more emotional departure from Southampton.

As streamers linked the sides of the SS Chusan with the grim, crane-lined docks, the tears flowed. And amid her own Anne noticed that her father, not a man given to weeping in public, was crying. Anne and John stood on the ship's rail, clutching their baby, and wondering whether they would return to England. 'My father was only in his sixties but I was really concerned that I might not see him again,' Anne said.

As the ship pulled into Southampton Water Anne and John made their way to their small cabin to be seasick for three days. Anne was expecting their second child. Janet, however, enjoyed the trip. At eighteen months, she revelled in the facilities of the nursery with its rocking horse and kiddies' swimming pool.

In Singapore the couple had their patience tested again as the OMF officials prayed with them and talked over the possibilities for their future work. Tribal work in the Philippines was one option, another was work in Indonesia (then at war). A third possibility was work in Thailand.

Called into the office of the General Director, Oswald Sanders, they faced the white-haired veteran missionary whose quiet, gentle manner had already endeared him to them. Under the whirling fan, against a background of books and potted plants, the Director gave them his decision: Manorom, a fairly large mission hospital that practised modern medicine and whose superintendent and wife had been students with Anne's parents. Relief seeped through the couple as readily as perspiration from the clammy heat. One of the doctors at Manorom had been on Anne and John's prayer list and, because they had done plenty of homework on the appointments they could have been offered, they already knew a lot about the work there.

Manorom was the decision: but it was to be some months before they arrived. First came language training, because now the couple had to learn Thai—a tonal language, similar in some ways to Chinese. They both got on well—John because he was good at hearing sounds and mimicking, and Anne because she could analyse the language well. But Anne did have one major difficulty: a naturally shy person who was always frightened of looking foolish, she was afraid to speak out.

During this time it was again Janet who settled in the best, parading off to nursery school each morning, proudly wearing the yellow uniform Anne had made and carrying a wicker basket under her arm. The basket, however, didn't contain school books: it held a teddy bear and a potty—both of which the cheerful toddler refused to be without.

It was while they were in Singapore that David was born, and not long afterwards the family had to make the journey by cargo steamer to Bangkok. The three day journey was brightened for Janet when some of the sailors spread a tarpaulin over some boxes to create a miniature paddling pool. Bangkok brought home the realization of what they were in for. After sorting out the visas at the immigration department they walked into the streets of the city, to be plunged into a babble of noise and activity. 'It was frightening,' said Anne. 'At first I couldn't understand what was going on, or what people were saying.'

People thought the newcomers from Europe were odd too. There were no foreigners in Thailand at that time and Anne and John were often pinched by people wanting to know if they were real. The Thai women were particularly fascinated by the children—grabbing handfuls of flesh to see if they were any different to the white plastic dolls on sale in the market. John had another problem: Thai men had no hair on their arms and his arms were continually being plucked by curious old ladies.

For twelve months the family lived in the country, sharing a Thai-style wooden house with a senior missionary, while studying the language eight hours a day, five days a week. A boy who had recently finished school spent three hours a day with them and, using the principles taught by the language school, the couple gradually began to piece the language together and get more proficient. Anne had a sleepless night the first time she realized she was going to have to use the language alone. One evening the senior missionary told her that the following morning she was to go to the village post office and get a stamp: 'I had never been so frightened as then,' she admitted. She walked into the post office the next day and joined the queue—the only foreigner. As she reached the counter and spoke to the khaki-clad official behind the grill she suddenly realized he was passing over a stamp of the right denomination. 'The triumph of having gone and come back with the stamp I wanted was marvellous.'

A year later, and language training over, Anne, John, Janet and David moved to Manorom Hospital where they knew their work for God was to begin. Even then it wasn't quite time to start: both Anne and John had to study for the Thai medical examinations since their English medical degrees were not valid in Thailand. So it was back to basics with written exams followed by a return trip to Bangkok for oral exams which they took in Thai since their ability to use it created a bond of interest.

Manorom Hospital was three blocks of white cement buildings, each three storeys high and raised on cement posts ten feet off the ground as a protection during the months of the year when the river banks overflowed and the area was flooded.

The tiny house that Anne and John moved into was also on stilts—spindly poles that held the wooden structure well above the wet season's danger level. It was probably all there was to commend the corrugated iron roofed home—a minute kitchen-cum-bathroom and two rooms were all they had. They hung up a woven mat to divide their bedroom into two areas, one for the children and one for themselves. But it was several months before they found out what it was that brought tears when they took David to bed, and made him sleep so restlessly. The discovery was made when Anne eventually realized why the mosquito net covering the baby's bed was ragged along the side that hung by the wall . . . it was chewed during a nightly visitation from rats.

And if the house was rough, the approach road was just as bad: it was a dirt track, ending in two long planks that stretched the last forty feet to the base of the house. This demanded a tough balancing trick for a mother laden down with two infants plus bicycle! The planks were needed, however. They were only inches above a bog. To make matters even more uncomfortable, the leprosy wing of the hospital was just a few yards from the house.

For almost a year they existed in this wooden shack—the worst house they were ever expected to live in with Anne working two hours a day in the hospital while John looked after the children, and Anne taking the lion's share of baby-sitting duties while John worked. She created a pattern that helped get the children out of the confines of the house and provided a welcome test for her growing fluency with the Thai language. Each afternoon she balanced the children on the cycle she had bought and rode Thai style into the village—David perching on a tiny seat behind the handlebars and Janet singing with delight as she sailed along, surveying the countryside from her seat on the luggage carrier. The half-mile ride to the village took the children to the play area and Anne to the village store where she bought a bottle of Coke and chatted to the locals: 'It made me use the language in a non-threatening situation.' Any errors with the language soon found Anne or John with ready tutors in the shape of Janet. The children's Thai grew more rapidly than their parents'.

For two years life ticked along at Manorom with Anne and John adapting to a missionary hospital situation. Then they were asked to look after a small clinic in the middle of nowhere. With Anne expecting their third child, it was a frightening thought. The village could be isolated by flood-water for long periods of time if it rained heavily. Anne said, 'It challenged our faith, knowing I would be unable to reach a bigger hospital if it were needed.' As it happened, they were joined by Dr Catherine Maddok— the wife of the superintendent at Manorom—and Catherine delivered the third baby safely. Anne and John named the little boy Christopher after Catherine's husband—one of the tangible ways in which Anne was able to show her appreciation for all that the couple had done for them.

Work in the clinic made John realize that he ought to know more on the surgical side of medicine, so when they returned to Manorom he began to study surgery with a view to becoming a Fellow of the Royal College of Surgeons. The long hours of study, plus his busy days in the hospital, meant that Anne was left alone with just the children for company for long periods. But her busy nature refused to accept idleness. She had always been an avid reader and friends in England had often sent piles of magazines and books which she devoured at a great rate. She became fascinated with the way writers used words to conjure up pictures. But it was a flash of anger that set her off writing for herself.

An article in the Christian magazine *Crusade* made missionaries seem like holy people, set apart, and touched in some special way by God. 'I was provoked to write a reply—something I had never done before,' Anne explained. She was sure that her letter to the editor, David Winter, was destined for the wastepaper bin. But it appeared in the magazine. So encouraged was Anne that she continued to write, and eventually asked David's advice about writing professionally. Wisely he suggested she sign on for a correspondence course in journalism—a secular course. The wisdom of that advice soon became clear as Anne began to unravel the mysteries of words under the guidance of the London School of Journalism. Writing Christian material for non-Christian tutors prompted the replies: 'You may believe that—we don't. You are not convincing us.' So she began, for the first time, to consider how to write without the evangelical jargon that made up the usual editorial fare in Christian magazines.

It worked. More and more articles appeared in print— one of the conditions of the course. And as editors saw her name they began to commission material. Eventually Anne saw an advertisement for a new type of Scripture Union note and tried her hand. It was when she was on furlough in England with the family that she happened to meet and discuss her writing with Scripture Union's then book editor, Michael Hews. He asked whether she had ever considered writing a book. Michael also had the germ of an idea, suggesting Anne's experiences as a new missionary. The result was *Once Bitten*—now reprinted as *Missionary Without Pretending*. It was an honest appraisal of missionary work, written realistically, with Anne herself featuring as the 'heroine' Jenny Thorne. All the situations had actually happened to Anne.

Anne was to discover that Christians, on the whole, didn't respond well to truth in writing. Asked by a Christian newspaper to write other material she sent a batch of articles she had not previously shown to anyone. The frankness and honesty of the material was unlike anything in print at that time—and earned Anne a quick response. She got her articles back with a covering note saying that the editor only wanted readers to know about missionary doctors' successes—not their failures. That comment made Anne think very carefully. No matter how hard she prayed she couldn't escape the feeling that God wanted her to be truthful and realistic. She hadn't had that letter long when *Once Bitten* was published and to her amazement, one senior missionary said to Anne: 'Surely it couldn't have been that bad?' Anne listed all the other things she had *not* written about—and the protest ended. In fact the book drew little flak. 'People don't worry too much about a missionary working in the rice fields of Thailand who's just written her first book.' But it was to be a milestone. Gradually God directed Anne into an amazing change of lifestyle.

She was asked by OMF to use two days a week to write for them, and help produce materials in the Thai language for people who were functionally illiterate. Faced with that challenge, Anne set about studying how others tackled the same problem: the Family Planning Association for example, who produced superb literature that communicated their message to people who could barely read. As Anne honed and sharpened her skills with the typewriter she began to spend less time with her stethoscope round her neck. Eventually she planned to write full-time—Thai materials and other helpful articles and publications— but events robbed her of that opportunity.

Anne and John were in England on furlough after about fourteen years in Thailand when a series of catastrophies in which friends died caused Anne to think more seriously about death. But worse was to come. One weekend the whole family were together at their furlough flat in Haywards Heath. The children, usually at boarding school, were on holiday, and it was a peaceful, happy time for Anne. But then suddenly the telephone rang to bring a cloud to all their lives. Five adult missionary friends and seven children had died in a road accident near their Thailand home. Five out of eight missionary families at Manorom whom Anne had left just a few months before had been bereaved. The 9,000 miles distance couldn't reduce the awful sadness. It was obvious that John should return immediately for two weeks—he was the medical superintendent and would be needed desperately both for his medical expertise and his pastoral care. Anne was needed, too. Her own professional training was required in the hospital. Her writing must take a back seat.

On the furlough following the tragedy, Anne became convinced that they should stay in England. The children, whose young lives had been shattered by the accident, needed their parents. Anne, too, needed the security of knowing they were safe and that John would be home at nights. But John still felt that Manorom was where they should be. They went back, after struggling for a year with their conflicting emotions. All Anne could do was agree to be a supportive wife and trust God. Within a year of their return John was in the operating theatre one day when he sensed God telling him their time in Thailand was over. It was a simple as that. Six weeks later they returned to England.

Back in England they had no work, no home, and little money. However, friends had agreed to continue to support the children in boarding schools for a few months. Five days after arriving in the country, Anne and John decided to look up an old friend, George Hoffman at TEAR Fund. George had visited their home in Thailand and they had helped on a number of TEAR Fund projects. TEAR Fund, meanwhile, had supported some of OMF's work. But they did not expect the result they got when they walked into the mission's offices in Teddington—John came out with the invitation to be full time medical consultant for TEAR Fund.

They rented a house a few miles away in New Malden, Surrey, and Anne looked for work herself. She didn't fancy the idea of becoming a medical practitioner again—it meant working nights, weekends and awkward hours, which defeated the whole object of returning to look after her three growing children. After church one day she idly looked through the *Church of England Newspaper* and for the first time found her eyes drawn to the situations vacant column. *Buzz* magazine were advertising for a sub-editor. Anne didn't know what *Buzz* was—or what a sub-editor did—but since it involved magazine work she telephoned about the job. The post had been taken.

Five days later her phone rang. The voice at the other end said that *Buzz's* publishing editor, Peter Meadows, would like to meet Anne, whom he knew about from her articles. Later, in the upstairs room which served him as an office, they chatted together about the magazine. Peter told Anne that *Buzz* had acquired the *Life of Faith* magazine and was planning to turn it into a magazine for Christian families. An extra pair of hands was needed temporarily—was she interested? The answer had to be yes. Anne knew that God wanted her to write, perhaps this was the opening she needed. She was appointed editorial assistant but some weeks later had a further shock. Called into Peter's office again, at ten o'clock one morning, she discovered that the editor would be leaving and the board had unanimously told Peter to invite Anne to be editor of the new *Family* magazine.

'It will help everyone if I can have an answer by lunchtime—but I will understand if you do need more time,' said Peter. Anne didn't need the concession. She was always ready to tackle a fresh challenge, and knew that John would be supporting her. She sensed God saying, 'This is the thing I have been nudging you into all along. Go ahead and try it. You know nothing about it but trust me to see you through.'

On her own, with no secretary, and with her assistant editor, though appointed, working out a two months' notice at another job, Anne worked late and long to produce the *Life of Faith* each month and plan for the September launch of the new *Family* magazine. They were exciting days. A breakfast launch in a top London hotel introduced Anne to a new range of people—and introduced the new magazine to them. Then came the moment when the first issue rolled off the press. Anne went with Peter to the printers in Sussex to see the first copies appear. But as she watched the pages hurtling from the printing press she saw what all editors dread—a black square appearing where a photograph should have been. It was a printing error but it didn't take away the devastation of the moment. To make matters worse, the picture that should have appeared was of the Queen.

'It was all I could see. It was awful,' she said. She soon put that behind her, though, as *Family* magazine began to carve a name for itself in Christian life in Britain. Anne's medical experience was invaluable in highlighting some of the social and psychological issues behind Christian needs. And the hospitality she had shown people for years reaped a harvest of writers who had an intimate knowledge of many of the more complex subjects she wanted to tackle.

With giant leaps of faith she found herself helping to organize Royal Week—a camping holiday for 4,000 Christians in Cornwall—as well as encouraging the setting up of help groups to give assistance to Christians with all kinds of problems. Largely through the challenge of the magazine, single parents were inspired to join the Christian Link Association for Single parents. Couples who had lost infants in cot deaths heard of support groups. Readers were challenged to pray for their children's schools. Very many issues were tackled as Anne became more and more proficient in the use of words and mastered the skills of editing, sub-editing, and managing the day-to-day affairs of a magazine with a rising circulation.

She also became a popular speaker at large conventions—including Filey week and the Spring Harvest holiday conference held in North Wales. Anne the editor, became the person more and more people turned to for help and advice on many of the basic dilemmas of Christian family life. At this time she developed a growing friendship with Lyndon Bowring and Charlie Colchester who had become directors of CARE Trust and CARE Campaigns—the one-time Festival of Light born out of a desire to demonstrate that Christian principles and values need to be upheld in Britain and to fight against the rotting moral values of the country. (The initials CARE stand for Christian Action, Research and Education.) Anne had been a trustee of CARE for some time when the two men presented a new challenge to her. After four years at *Family*, Lyndon and Charlie challenged her: 'Anne we believe God wants you to *do* some of the things you *write* about. We want you to join us and start doing things.' Anne smiled—and politely refused. She was enjoying her editing, and for her the typewriter and sub-editing pen seemed to be more powerful instruments than any she could find at CARE Trust.

The men were undismayed. 'We still believe this is what God wants and you are the person God wants. Do you mind if we leave it for the time being and see if God tells you what we believe he has told us?'

Nothing happened for six months. Anne considered it but could think of too many excuses. 'I was then forty-six, enjoying my job with *Family,* and too old to start pioneering again. It was time to put my feet up and let someone younger tackle the fresh challenges.' At Easter 1984 she was again at Spring Harvest, sitting on the main platform during an evening meeting, watching the back of Jim Graham's head as his soft Scottish voice preached about Moses. 'I began to realize that the excuses Moses had given were identical to the ones I was giving. I began to identify with what Jim was saying. I knew that God was speaking to me directly.' And as the white-haired preacher challenged anyone who had heard God speaking to them to stand, he didn't realize that behind him, on the platform, Anne was on her feet. 'I stood because I actually wanted to make it clear to myself, so that I would not forget that God had spoken to me.'

Afterwards Anne went to the chalet of Lyndon and his wife Celia and prayed and rejoiced with them over a bottle of wine! It was the fulfilment of their dream. Six months later she moved to the cramped basement office in Down Street, Mayfair, where she faced the massive challenge of setting up a network of Christian families all over Britain who would take into their homes people in need. 'Everything else I have done culminates in this challenge,' Anne believes. 'It is one that needs the knowledge I gained while practising medicine . . . the editorial skills I picked up writing . . . the recognition of so many needs which I saw from *Family* magazine . . . and the drive to put them all together to produce positive, solid Christian help.'

She started, as she had done five years previously on *Family,* with no secretary, and long hours curled up at home working nights in her sleeping bag, with papers strewn on the floor around her while she scribbled notes. For Anne Townsend it was another, fresh challenge, the third in her forty-eight years. As he had always done, God was building upon her past experience. Now she was planning to devote her time to discovering at least two hundred caring homes in the first year alone. She was also the editor of all CARE Trust and CARE Campaign's literature—which in itself inspires thousands to pray and take practical measures to protect the unborn, the young and family life in Britain.

All her life Anne has been a fighter. Now she faces her toughest battle, but does so with the experience of two other careers and a God who has never let her down.

4

PRADIP SUDRA

From the Banks of the Ganges to the Backstreets of Britain

The huge brass bell hanging in the sheltered, shuttered, side temple off the main Hindu temple fascinated little Pradip Sudra. Its noise, bold and echoing, elevated it into the realms of the gods standing stone-faced inside the temple itself. It was ironic that that bell, part of the Hindu ritual, should turn out to be the very instrument through which the young Indian boy was to be put off his native religion.

Pradip was born in Kenya after his grandparents had moved to East Africa in the early 1920s. Belonging to the caste second only to the Brahmin priests, the family were builders and Pradip's father helped build schools, hospitals, and prisons—anything, in fact, that needed his craftsman's skills. The family decided to stay in Africa, and it was in the small town named Kisumu on Lake Victoria, that Pradip grew up.

Life, for the youngster was fun. It centred on the temple with its huge community feast days when several thousand would pack the enormous hall. Especially exciting were the days of Navratri when for nine days and nine nights dancing and entertainment brought the crowds to the temple precincts.

'I loved it,' he said. 'Some people danced and the rest of us watched and stood around talking and meeting relatives. It was a great social event.'

Inside the main area of the temple the gods stared blankly into space. Every day Pradip would stand in front of the statues, hands folded, bow and contemplate, sometimes watching the priest ceremonially wash the figures. Food—mainly sweetmeats—was offered to the idols and then given to the people worshipping.

And all the while the big bell hung temptingly in the small adjacent temple dedicated to the god Shankar. One afternoon, when most of the adults were sleeping, resting from the heat of the African sun, Pradip, his sister and a cousin, crept into the open side temple, and carefully poking their bare toes into the shutters, climbed among the rafters and began to push the bell until it started to ring. Chuckling with glee they hung and pushed and watched the enormous object of their energy swing backwards and forwards, uttering its enormous 'bong' as the shutter clanged against the side.

Suddenly the priest, angry at being woken from his siesta, appeared at the base of the bell, roaring and shouting at the trio. Boiling with rage, he swore and cursed the children, sending them back to their homes, each with a cuff across the ear. Small as he was, Pradip began to have doubts about the faith. 'I was disillusioned by his swearing and anger. I wondered how he could be a priest,' he recounted. From that point he began to see the idols as mere stone, created by human hands. 'How can they be gods?' he puzzled.

Finishing his primary education, Pradip moved on to a secondary school, owned by a Muslim friend of his father. It was then that a different religion entered his youthful mind—Christianity. For the school, under the influence of the British Education Act, had to provide religion and that meant either Islam, because it was a Muslim school—

or Christianity, but not the Hinduism into which he had been born. Pradip could not speak Arabic—the language of Islam—but did speak English, so he elected to learn Christianity.

He was twelve-and-a-half when he made his tentative excursions into Christianity—the Old Testament stories, the sermon on the mount and the book of Acts. He was not interested in the subject but it seemed an easy way to boost his 'O' level chances. There were, however, other influences. Christianity was taught in the school by an American missionary, and he invited the youngsters to his home for a regular youth evening with fun, games and an epilogue. The missionary also ran camping holidays under canvas or occasionally in a school near Nairobi. Pradip may have nurtured doubts about his own religion since his bell-ringing exploit, but he had more serious doubts about Christianity: doubts that increased when a school friend, Hitash, became a Christian. Pradip and others enjoyed calling him names and completely cut him off from their company. Their favourite name for Hitash was a Gujarati word which means 'he has been nailed'—a parallel with Christianity which he would think about in later years.

One day at school the teacher-missionary read from John's gospel Jesus' words, 'I am the way and the truth and the life. No-one comes to the father except through me,' and Pradip was angry inside. 'How can one person claim direct access to God when my own religion and probably Islam are just as good?' he demanded. As he questioned he began to look into his own Hindu faith more seriously; and the more he studied it the more he began to be drawn away from it and towards the central figure of Christianity—Jesus Christ. One of his key influences was not the Bible but the Vedic scripture (the old Hindu religious writings) on sacrifice. It talked about a perfect sacrifice for man—and the more he read the more he realized that those scriptures were fulfilled in Jesus. 'I was very much drawn to Christianity,' he admitted.

But he refused to make his growing faith common
knowledge. Each day he would smuggle his Scripture
Union Bible notes from their hiding place among his text
books and read, always afraid of what his parents might
say, and always aware of what had happened to his former
friend when he had become a Christian. What helped
Pradip in his struggle to be a Christian was that a number
of his friends had made the same decision—in fact they
apologized to Hitash for laughing at him—and the most
decisive factor was that his father had gone to England a
few months before to prepare for the family to live there.

Having no father about took the main pressure off the
shoulders of the young fourteen-year-old when he finally
decided to become a Christian. Even so, there were still
moments when his mother or relatives would bring a sickening feeling to Pradip's stomach as they questioned him
about his regular involvement with the Christians. 'Sometimes, when confronted by my family with the claim that I
was a Christian I denied it. I told them I was not. I was so
ashamed afterwards, it hurt.'

His mother thought he would grow out of his involvement with Christianity when they moved to England,
away from the influence of his Christian friends. Two days
before coming to England Pradip was in a nearby town
speaking to missionary friends of the American. Stanley
Davis, now president of the Evangelical Missionary Alliance, was working there. He learned of Pradip's move and
as soon as he heard the town they were to go to—Crawley—reached into his pocket, took out a diary, and scribbled down the address of his uncle who was secretary of
the local Free Church in that town.

Four days later, walking around Crawley to get his
bearings, Pradip noticed the name of the road where the
church secretary lived. He fished the paper from his
pocket, checked the name, and rang the bell. When he

spoke to Stanley Davis' uncle he was promised that the youth leader would come and see him. It was one of Pradip's parents' biggest surprises when Rob White knocked at the door later the same day and introduced himself to Pradip. They couldn't understand how, when they had hardly established themselves in England, their son should have friends calling so soon.

The youth fellowship at the church encouraged Pradip to attend other meetings, but his family believed it was simply a phase he would grow out of.

At school he was academically brilliant, gobbling up twelve 'O' levels and four 'A' levels and then winning a sponsorship in an apprenticeship as an electrical engineer. For a year at South Kent College in Dover, followed by three years with Rolls Royce and Derby College of Further Education, he studied and directed his attention towards a successful career. Because of the sponsorship, he had money to spend and he managed to get home most weekends to meet his growing number of friends at church. During the week he would occasionally visit churches near the college.

A shy person, Pradip found it difficult to break through the English reserve and because he was career-minded his spiritual life took a back seat. 'I grew very little spiritually in those years,' he admits. Though certain about his Christian faith, he was not committed to growth in his spiritual life. Away from home, however, and without the fears which had previously worried him of being thrown out of the family, he decided to be baptized. There was some opposition from his parents—baptism was considered to be a mystical, curious ceremony—and they refused to attend the service. But even baptism didn't give his faith the impetus it needed.

The apprenticeship was followed by a job in the electricity supply industry. It was a well-paid, important job into which he sunk himself in an effort to be successful.

He was then able to live at home, and he settled down to enjoy life at the church. But as he progressed and began to taste success at work things started to change in the youth group at the church. Many of the young people were claiming to have been filled with the Holy Spirit. Pradip watched and one evening spent time praying with friends and had an experience of being filled with the Spirit. That was enough, he thought. Many of the young people were speaking in tongues, but he considered that completely unnecessary in his own case: 'I spoke six languages—English, Swahili, Gujarati, Hindi, Punjabi and Urdu—that seemed enough for me. It was certainly enough to praise God with.' God didn't agree—within weeks he was finally given release and spoke in tongues. 'It was a wonderful experience, and certainly the language bore no comparison to any language I knew,' he said.

Pradip's faith had changed him gradually over the years. At home he had been cautious about speaking of his activities; at college he had felt free to enter into the work of local churches because his family knew little of what he was doing. But living at home again he began to realize the pain his father felt. His father complained that one of his sons was not conforming, and he was right. Pradip had made it clear that the Hindu custom of arranged marriages was not for him, and he had no intention of following Hindu practices. In a large family—six sisters and three brothers—and in a culture where the family meant everything, it was tantamount to cutting himself off. The Asian community cared for each other and the role of the wider family was integral to the culture. It was accepted without question that children, parents and relatives were taken care of.

Pradip now began to feel that the local fellowship to which he belonged, the Vine Fellowship, which had begun when a number of people had split from the Crawley Church, were his family. Ties were fastened that were never to be undone. He began to feel an affinity towards the members of the fellowship that distance and time would not block.

Despite a growing love for the fellowship, his main ambitions were still directed towards his career in the electricity industry. In 1979, at the age of twenty-five, he managed to get one of the status symbols for which he had been striving: a new car. Gleaming red, it was his joy. Inside a few weeks, however, the car was wrecked as a drunken driver smashed into him head on, demolishing the vehicle and leaving Pradip wondering at the miracle which merely saw him shocked for a couple of days. 'I only had a little mark on my little finger,' he said. It was a crash that could have ended his life—instead it changed it.

For two days his mind replayed the incident and Pradip began to question God. 'I wondered why he had saved me, why I was still alive when I had no right to be.' As he lobbed his questions heavenward, God answered. The answer came first in a verse from the prophet Jeremiah: 'My people have committed two sins: They have forsaken me, the spring of living water, and have dug their own cisterns, broken cisterns that cannot hold water' (Jeremiah 2:13). A picture came into Pradip's mind as he read. He saw again the house where he had lived in Kenya and the huge clay water jugs that were part of every home which held refreshing water. He saw his Indian people picking up the pots and attempting to drink but as the pot was raised the water sprayed from holes and cracks all round the broken pot. He felt God speaking to him: 'That is a picture of your people, good religious people, trying to drink out of religion that doesn't satisfy.' The career-minded young man started to think seriously about the claims of God on his own life—and the power of the gospel on the lives of his own people.

While he was thinking, the insurance company replaced his new car—and he offered to give Rob White a lift to

Norfolk. Rob was to be interviewed for the position of Assistant Director of British Youth for Christ. After the drive to the YFC training centre, then in Brecklands, Norfolk, Pradip sat waiting while Rob was being interviewed. Another YFC worker, Mike Morris started to chat to him, and once he had discovered Pradip's background, explained the need in England for someone to help with the cross-cultural evangelism that was now necessary in a multi-culture country. Previously, Mike explained, missionaries had gone abroad: now YFC was wanting someone to come from abroad who understood the different cultures and could encourage Christians in Britain to reach out to immigrants in a non-threatening but effective way.

He pointed out that when the second chapter of Acts talked of starting in Jerusalem, and moving out to Samaria and other parts of the world it did not intend the workers in Jerusalem to be Jewish or the Samaritans to reach only Samaria. 'Our job,' Mike enthused, 'is to reach all British young people with the gospel—whatever their background.'

Youth for Christ badly needed an adviser who would encourage others in such an outreach ministry—teaching workers in schools, youth groups, inner-city and other areas, the best methods of reaching others. It was an interesting talk and since he had nothing else to do Pradip listened. Only later, in the privacy of his home, did the words begin to have a deep effect. As he prayed and gave more consideration to the thoughts that were beginning to percolate into his mind, he asked YFC for more details. After an interview of his own, Pradip and YFC sensed that their paths were crossing.

Fearful that he had misunderstood the guidance, Pradip shared his fears—and hopes—with the elders of his fellowship. They encouraged him to continue looking in the direction of YFC. Formal interviews followed, but still he hedged when it came to the question of joining because he was becoming more aware of how ill-trained he was for that type of ministry. Pradip's experience was limited to leading a house group and occasional preaching and giving testimonies. To head a major cross-cultural work was something that needed a great deal of training. So he suggested waiting for a year while he went abroad for training. YFC agreed and Pradip gave up his job to join Operation Mobilisation. He chose that organization because the previous year he had heard the leader, George Verwer, speaking about the challenge of missions and particularly short-term possibilities. He remembered enough of the talk to know where he could get the training he needed. Although the training in India was normally for a minimum of two years, because of Pradip's Asian background and his future job with YFC, Operation Mobilisation agreed to take him for a year. He started off with some training in Britain and Belgium—learning the OM philosophies, and about cultural aspects of work overseas, as well as spending time in prayer and Bible study. Finally there came the plane ride from Paris to Delhi.

The sights, sounds and smells of Delhi riveted the Asian Christian. 'I couldn't get over the sight and sounds of India—Indians in the airport wearing flip-flops and pyjamas, and the heat and chaos of the international airport. And then when our party of about thirty left the airport I was surrounded by beggars. I had been used to beggars in Kenya but in Africa they sat peacefully asking for money and waiting for you to go to them. Here they clamoured round, harassing us.'

Rob Sinclair, a Canadian, met the party and ushered them over to a battered old Thames Trader van. As they struggled over the tailboard Pradip gave a helping hand to the girls in the party, pushing luggage and people further into the interior of the van until it moved off, with its cargo of people sitting astride suitcases, rucksacks and bags. A week of training and orientation in a local school followed. Sleeping on the floor, wrapped only in his sleeping bag, Pradip discovered a harder life. Food was cooked over open fires covered by large stones and huge simmering pots. The common diet was rice, a curry and chapatis. Teaching and training in the mornings was followed in the afternoons by practical language training on the streets of the city. Pradip watched as his new OM colleagues tried to learn short phrases in Hindi and then practice them in real conversations on the streets.

Pradip was himself learning about Indian practices like bartering in the shops—and driving. He regularly drove the transit van to and from central points, a hair-raising experience. 'I had not had to stop on a dual carriageway before for a cart being pulled by a slow-moving buffalo, or cows and goats ambling aimlessly along. Then there were the hundreds of dogs, acting as if they owned the road, and people who walked across when and where they liked.'

After a fortnight in Delhi he was moved on to Lucknow, the capital city of the Utter Pradish state, where OM had their Indian training base. A week later he was sent with a team of eight in the same old Thames Trader van which had collected him from the airport, to the holy city of the Hindus—Varanasi, on the banks of the holy River Ganges.

Six Indian men, one Swiss man, and Pradip made up that evangelistic team, sent into the city which was the heartbeat of the religion into which he had been brought up and later set aside in favour of life-changing faith in Jesus Christ. Living in one tiny room, sleeping on the floor, and cooking their own primitive meals, was an experience unique to Pradip, and, as all eight found, it was a time not just of ministry but of adjustment and learning about each other. 'It was not easy living together twenty-four hours a day, doing all the work, and chores—including washing by hand.'

The tailgate of the van became their pulpit and book-shop as they toured the area singing to get an audience and then breaking into a few short testimonies or mini-sermons before selling Bibles, New Testaments, Gospels or other Christian books and literature. The group lived on the income from the material they sold, but they had no problem in selling to the seekers after religion who frequented the holy city. In a good week 1,000 New Testaments went as eager buyers packed the tailgate. 'It seemed they were anxious to buy anything to read. I was surprised to see how many people bought New Testaments and Gospels but I guess it was part of the nature of the Indians that they should want religious materials. India is probably one of the most religious countries in the world, and there is no gulf between religion and life. If people prosper in business they feel it is because God has prospered them—the two things go together.'

The group preached anywhere, alongside the river, by the road, in the market, anywhere where they could draw a crowd—not a difficult task. Pradip's first real test came as the team dropped the tailgate in the street one after-noon. A Hindu guru watched them prepare and before they had announced who they were began to call out, cursing and swearing, saying he wanted nothing to do with these people. 'I sensed strongly that it was an attack of the devil,' said Pradip. 'I prayed and told him to "shut up in the name of Jesus", and he did. For the whole duration of the meeting he was quiet. I felt for the first time in India the promise of God being fulfilled in me, and the power and authority he was giving me in his name.'

The mighty River Ganges presented Pradip with his first realization of the lostness of humanity. Early one morning he went to the water's edge and saw the funeral pyres of up to 200 bodies being cremated. The stench of human flesh, and the horrific sight of the flames eating into the bodies, with crowds of people watching gripped him. 'I saw the intense lostness of man and the stranglehold the enemy had upon him. But even as I watched and began to despair I realized that I had the answer, and it was an answer I simply had to share with people.'

That experience was to be the motivating factor in Pradip's life. He moved on to Gujarat, the state in which Ghandi had been born, to work with a church-planting team under the guidance of the indigenous Friends Missionary Prayer Band. It was a time of rapid growth in his own Christian experience and character. The work was with native people in villages with some Christian influence, helping encourage growth in the church and teaching the Christians as well as preaching and evangelizing outsiders. The simple faith of the villagers impressed Pradip. He saw hundreds come to know Jesus Christ in a real way as the team, along with an independent evangelist, witnessed and preached. Miracles occurred regularly, enlarging his faith even more. Personal miracles—the group slept one night by the roadside and woke to discover tigers' footprints all round the places their bodies had lain; and miracles of healing, as when he saw a woman who had been ill for five years healed instantly, rise from the bed and prepare a meal. A little baby who had not stopped crying for days suddenly smiled and was cured.

It was a dramatic introduction to the miraculous, but Pradip's time in India was due to end—his eight month spell with OM was almost over. A letter from Youth for Christ in England, however, complicated his plans. For a change of leadership which had now put his old friend Rob White into the director's post had also led to a switch in training methods which meant that the new timetable would begin in January of the following year—not September as previously. Pradip was invited to spend the three spare months in India, visiting the Youth for Christ work there. He jumped at the chance—an opportunity to begin to work with the organization he was going to join and also see their work in India.

He was invited to visit ten centres and spend a few days in each. When he arrived at the first base, however, he was to discover that through some misinterpretation of the letters, they had understood him to be an experienced evangelist from England, and had a full range of services planned.

Pradip didn't dare point out the mistake. They had been told he was a big evangelist—he would try to preach like one. It was a nerve-wracking, but exciting three months. Sharpened by the open-air preaching he had done with OM, and with his Bible knowledge deepened by daily Bible studies—many of which he had led—he made up parables to illustrate his talks. These, he had discovered, gave him an instant entré into the Indian mind-set. He might not have felt like a famous evangelist but the small, Asian man now aged twenty-nine, began to reap the harvest that had been prepared by the YFC workers of the past. In schools, colleges and universities, in the open-air, door-to-door, and in public meetings, thousands of Indian men, women and children, came to the Lord in those three months. If the preacher needed any indication from God that his future ministry was with his own people, he had his final lesson on the dusty streets and official buildings of the land his parents had left so many years before.

His incredible experiences over, Pradip returned to England and British Youth for Christ. His real work was now to begin. There was one problem he had to overcome first: an enlarged liver that was giving him pain and causing the medical authorities concern. In his year in India Pradip had remained free from the sicknesses that had sometimes afflicted his colleagues. The dull, uninspired food had bored him—but not harmed him. Now in England he was taken to hospital for a fortnight for tests. In the isolation ward, boredom was setting in when the doctors told him he could leave. Whatever had been harming his liver had gone. He was cured—and they couldn't understand it. He left willingly and made for Norfolk and YFC training. For two months he learnt the background of YFC and its methods of operation, meeting workers from all over the country. He also spent time researching the districts of high Asian population and visiting Christian organizations operating in those areas to see what was being done. He had an open brief: it was a new job and he was travelling on uncharted waters.

He now lives in a small ground-floor flat in Wolverhampton, on the north-western outskirts of Birmingham. His neat black beard and moustache frame his swarthy complexion. He walks with a limp, the product of having one leg slightly shorter than the other since an accident when he was two. Stockily built, but not tall, Pradip has a gentle voice and calm manner.

Cardboard boxes act as filing cabinets—a tribute to his naturally neat instincts and meticulous approach to his work. He has not been long in the flat so another two cardboard boxes form an impromptu table for the television set in the corner.

The lounge is neat, with the plain walls broken by two paintings—one framed in plain, cream wood, showing a sunset shafting through trees and with a text underneath, 'Your God will be your glory' (Isaiah 60:19). On the opposite wall in an ornate gilt frame is an old man, bearded, leaning praying over a table spread sparsely with bread, a bowl of soup and a Bible. It is somehow a fitting picture for the wall of a man who, as a bachelor, knows the problems of preparing and eating food—but ensures that his Bible is always handy. And handy it is; neatly positioned on the edge of the table alongside the files, writing paper and rows of pens that are a tribute to the early morning start he gives his work.

The flat itself is on the edge of an Asian community: the

best introduction to the work Pradip could have. His job title is short: evangelist. The work is vast—visiting mosques, schools and Asian centres to build relationships and learn about the cultural patterns and changes that Britain faces.

It is a delicate job, as tricky as walking a tightrope, needing an enormous amount of sensitivity together with the firmness and strength to be true to his calling. 'I want to provide living water to my people,' is his cry. He faces the restrictions of working within a system, and he needs wisdom to know when to challenge the system if it needs challenging. 'The approach of thirty years ago cannot be used today in a pluralistic society where Christians are in the minority,' he points out. 'Christ is the focus of all I do—but I need to be careful as I present him to Muslims, Asians, West Indians and Hindus.'

The size of the job is shown by the two million Asians in Britain. How can this short, cultured Asian Christian reach them? Even that is not the correct terminology: 'My job is to help and encourage others to reach them. Youth for Christ works only with local churches—we do not have the staff or the facilities to do it all ourselves.' But Pradip is well aware that in teaching others he must often end up doing it himself.

When he was in hospital a young Asian visited a white man in the next bed and began talking to Pradip. When Pradip left hospital he followed up the contact and the young man came to Christ, seeing something different in Pradip. It led to two other members of the same family becoming Christians—one a man in despair, an alcoholic in his twenties. He came to Pradip pleading to be prayed for—'He had heard that if Christians prayed for you things happen, he felt the love of God.'

Pradip believes that Asians in Britain have a cultural identity problem—and in some ways a crisis of identity in their religion, too. They face enormous problems if they become Christians—they risk being cut off from their families, banishment from their homes, and the loss of all friends and of the help of the close-knit Asian community. 'Many young people find it particularly difficult because they wonder who will marry them if they accept the Christian faith. It is a real problem.'

It is the local church's job to provide the security that will prevent Asians from being discouraged by those problems. He himself found in his local church—The Vine Fellowship—a replacement family. Churches need to consider the problems of poor housing, disadvantaged groups, and the inner-city dilemmas. He sees his challenge to be that of explaining to Christians that God's heart is 'with the poor of the nation'.

His first year, 1984, was one of laying a foundation of facts and information, and of building bridges. The next, 1985, was a year when he began to see the fulfilment of the work. He personally saw forty to fifty Asian people come to find Christ as the living water and believes that 'the credibility gap is closing' in many areas.

As in India Pradip is well aware that here in Britain he is 'reaping where others have sown'. Asian couples are coming to him for advice and counsel with their marriage problems—they are recognizing a deeper need and the one who can help them. He is only too well aware of the dangers: Hinduism accepts many gods. When Pradip became a Christian, a little statue of Jesus the Good Shepherd appeared on the family shrine among the other gods. But while Hindus accept any god, his job is to encourage them to seek and find the one God who can help—Jesus Christ.

The vision of the cracked African water pot lives with Pradip Sudra. He lives now not to plug the holes, but to put his own people in touch with the living water. He wants them to taste the same satisfying life he has discovered.

5

HILARY SMITH
The Copper Who Learned to Cry

'He's drunk; I'll do this one, Jimmy.' Hilary Smith began to wind down the window on the nearside of the white Ford Escort police car while the officer alongside her flicked the switch on the dashboard to set the blue light on the top of the car flickering.

Jimmy swung the car in a wide arc round Union Street, Aberdeen, in pursuit of the vehicle they had spotted crawling through the city centre. Down Market Street, towards the harbour, they went, turning right alongside the British Home Stores before accelerating alongside the other vehicle; as they did so Hilary waved her hand to halt their prey.

She gave a wry grin as the car stopped, reaching into her black standard-issue shoulder bag for her black plastic-covered notebook. Opening the door she turned towards the other vehicle, notebook in hand. Leaning down she tapped the driver's window and, as it rolled down, began to point out that she had the impression he might be drunk because of the slow speed at which he had been travelling. She invited the driver to leave his car and enter the police vehicle for a breath test.

The door opened. The driver's legs swivelled round until his feet touched the tarmac, and suddenly he collapsed, huge sobs convulsing his body. 'Jimmy,' Hilary called out, her two and a half years in the force not having prepared her for quite such a reception.

Her more experienced colleague hurried round, looked at the weeping figure and muttered to her: 'It's the dad of the wee bairn who's missing.' They took the distraught man to the police canteen, and there he unburdened himself. He had been driving and walking in a daze ever since his three-year-old daughter had disappeared three days earlier, searching for her ceaselessly.

As she realized the futility of the man's actions, and saw something of the sickening sense of loss he was feeling, Hilary's eyes filled with tears. 'God,' her heart and mind cried out, 'why do you let these things happen?' In the previous few months she had got on speaking terms with God. Her new life as a Christian had weakened the wall of resistance she had been building up as one of Aberdeen's policewomen. Since then she was more vulnerable. She hurt. She couldn't understand—but at least she could talk to God.

It was all very different from her former pattern of life.

She had been brought up to accompany her parents to a dull, lifeless Church of Scotland. Her memories were of the deadly boring Sunday School, interminable sermons rolling out over a yawning congregation, and rock-hard pews which had the ability to drive all feeling from her rear end within minutes. Her other religious feelings were bound up in two more solid items: a book and a chain. The book was a beautiful black and white illustrated treasury of Bible stories. Even as a ten-year-old Hilary had burst into tears of unhappiness when she opened the pages to see Jesus being crucified. 'It all seemed so unfair,' she said. The chain was a gift from a friend of her mother. The three sisters were invited to make a choice from three items of jewellery and Hilary grabbed the cross on its fine gold chain. 'I don't know why . . . it just appealed to me. With hindsight I can see that I was fascinated by biblical things.'

But all that was shattered when, at the age of ten, she watched the television pictures of Neil Armstrong gingerly reversing down the frail-looking ladder from his space craft. As she saw him set foot on the dusty surface of the moon, and heard those momentous words from outer space: 'A small step for man, a giant step for mankind,' the little Scottish girl's spirit took a giant step backwards.

'Suddenly I realized that the picture I had of God, surrounded by angels, perched in heaven, wasn't true. There was nothing out there but an enormous cavern of space, a vast emptiness.' In her youthful mind God died the day man reached the moon. Her Sound of Music dream of becoming a nun slipped into the background—along with the Bible given to her a couple of years before to mark regular church attendance.

Her parents, probably presuming that she was old enough to determine her own spiritual destiny, told her that the decision as to whether or not she went to church rested with her. That was all Hilary needed—church was now a thing of the past.

The family had moved about quite a bit as Hilary had grown up. Her favourite home being in the Shetland Islands, on the small community in Lerwick, where Father—a teacher—started to teach her French. When they moved back to the mainland, Forfar, Hilary was unhappy. The school was far larger than the island community she had grown to love and, shy as she was, she hated the new school, taking several months to settle down.

After 'O' levels she enrolled at a commercial college, taking a bi-lingual secretarial course—business French and German, along with shorthand, typing and office administration. From there she went on to Aberdeen University where she eventually gained an ordinary MA in advanced sociology and economic history. But if she earned educational qualifications her first spell of living away from home completed her education in other, more personal, areas of life.

She lived in the university halls of residence, perched on a hill overlooking the northern outskirts of the city, where her small room became a place of retreat for study, but all too often, also a retreat from the late-night entertainment she was beginning to enjoy. Pints of Black and Tan—a mixture of stout and bitter—became a staple diet, with discos, and late-night parties, her staple entertainment.

Any efforts to reach her made by the Christians on campus proved fruitless. She was not interested in the 'freshers' barbecue, organized by the Christian Union, and ignored Catriona, her neighbour in the halls, a shy introverted Christian. Nor did she want anything to do with the Bible studies and prayer meetings that were held in Catriona's room. Since Hilary was rarely in her room, they at least didn't disturb each other. The only concession to religion that Hilary made was the annual pilgrimage to church on Christmas Eve—and even then she called in at the pub first.

They were bad years. Ian, who had been Hilary's boyfriend for the past couple of years, was studying in Dundee. The two got engaged and began to see each other regularly at week-ends, often sleeping together. When Ian moved to London to continue his studies Hilary used the money her father gave her for travelling down to London. When her father discovered what his daughter was doing he was furious. He warned her: 'Hilary, you are not behaving like that on my money. Keep it up, and I stop sending you your allowance.' At nights her mother cried herself to sleep. But the threat paid off. At the time it rankled that, at the age of nineteen, her father still held the strings of her life, but in retrospect Hilary knew he had reacted in love and concern. She appreciated this even more when, as a policewoman, she saw the results of promiscuous behaviour in the lives of young offenders who had been allowed to go their own way without restraint.

Ian and Hilary re-evaluated their relationship and tried to back-pedal but, because he wasn't there when she needed to be close to him, and a substitute man just happened to be handy, she slipped into a double life. When Ian found out, the engagement was broken off. Unable to understand her own behaviour and riddled with remorse, one relationship led to another as she tried to compensate for the love she'd destroyed.

Those relationships had an effect on Hilary's personal life: 'I began to feel guilty—guilty because my parents didn't know, and guilty because I still loved Ian and had treated him badly.' It was to be years before that sense of guilt was exchanged for peace.

As the end of her university career drew near Hilary had to decide on her future. Any ideas of sitting behind a desk were rejected, despite that early commercial training. Her mother had been in the Women's Royal Navy— but the thought of wearing a uniform twenty-four hours a day and being tied to barracks and cut-off from the outside world didn't appeal.

It was while she was working in a supermarket as a holiday relief, stacking shelves and sitting at a cash-till checking up the endless supplies of shopping, that a new thought was born. One of the part-time workers was married to a policeman and occasionally he would appear at the shop. He would balance on one of the high stools in the compact staff room at the rear of the shop and delight the shop girls with stories of some of the funny sides of police life. But during those times Hilary began to question him in earnest. When he saw she was serious, he advised her to apply to the Metropolitan Police in London: 'It's too limited for a girl in the Scottish force,' he said. 'You'll have more opportunities in London.' Opportunity was what Hilary was seeking, so she sent off for application forms and returned them to Paddington Green, North London.

Crossing over the road from the underground station she saw the towering newly-built police station in front of her. Inside she met a couple of other hopeful girls and they were shown to the tidily designed single rooms in which they spent the night. Next morning all three faced the rigours of tests and examinations. A white-clad doctor gave them what, to Hilary, seemed a cursory medical—height, weight, eyesight, teeth—and then she faced an interview with the Superintendant—a man—and a lady Chief Inspector.

The Chief Inspector seemed intent on tripping Hilary. She asked whether any of Hilary's family had been in the force and getting a negative answer asked, 'Is it a career you will enjoy?' Then she flung another question across the table: 'Why did you apply to join through the usual channels, and not as a graduate entrant?' There was no answer. Hilary had not even realized there was a different approach. The graduate's entrance, she discovered later, led to an accelerated promotion after initial training.

It was not a good interview. Even so, the Scottish girl was bitterly disappointed later that day when she was called into the office of a more kindly woman officer and told her application had not been successful. She was advised to try again—as a graduate entrant—the following January. The stubborn will that had cut church and religion out of her life now reacted vehemently against London: she would try the Scottish Police Force.

The following morning she began telephoning. An interview in the careers section of the local force brought the advice that Northern or Grampian regions were both looking for female recruits. With no answer to her first phone call to the Northern region, Hilary requested application forms from Grampian, the force centred on Aberdeen. Not only did she get the forms—she got the job.

November 7th 1977, saw the bright-faced twenty-one-year-old arriving at Bucksburn B Division Headquarters and training department on the north-west side of the city of Aberdeen, for her first day in the police force. Armed with her suitcase, she joined the dozen or so other recruits—including three girls—facing a new career. After a morning behind the tables of a lecture room where they were given a basic understanding of the force, the different ranks and duties, and an insight into the training procedure, the twelve trailed out of the building to a waiting mini-bus to be taken on a tour of the divisional headquarters.

The van ride felt weird. 'We were still in civilian clothes and getting in and out of the van with its big police symbol on the side seemed strange. We could have been criminals,' recalled Hilary. The group was ferried to the divisional headquarters of C Division—one of the two city-centre divisions in Aberdeen. After a meal in the canteen, during which she felt self-conscious in her civilian clothes, Hilary was taken to a changing room by one of the female officers to find clothing (for which she had been measured at her August interview) neatly piled on a chair. The neat dark uniform, with its smart hat, seemed strange at first; strange but fulfilling. As she surveyed herself in the mirror and received the approval of the officer checking the measurements, Hilary was consumed with excitement. This was to be a new life.

As a probationer, Hilary would be accompanied during the next two years by a more senior officer, with a gradual reduction in the amount of supervision. She would also spend fourteen weeks at Tulliallan Police College. The men took delight in introducing her to the less exciting

aspects of the job. Douggie Ross, one of her early colleagues, led her scrambling through the tottering, crumb-
ling walls of partly demolished buildings to introduce her
to down-and-outs, watching them shove the bottles of
meths which were all they wanted from life, under their
tattered clothing as the officers appeared. Douggie took
her into the stinking stench of the hostel used by dirty,
drunken men in the city. He also treated her to stories of
Aberdeen's history from what proved to be an extensive
knowledge of the city.

Hilary found it difficult to overcome the nervousness
she had felt when she first left the central police station in
uniform. 'Suddenly I realized that once in uniform and
outside the station no one but I myself knew I had no
experience. To everyone else I was a cop—but I knew I
had no knowledge to show for the uniform. I felt a bit of a
phony.'

It was a feeling time would eventually erase, just as time
would give her the experience to overcome the fear she
had when first told she would have to appear in court.
Twice she sat, tense and nervous, in the police waiting-
room alongside the court without being called to give evidence. On the third occasion she was led to the witness
box, told to swear the oath, and asked to give her evidence. 'All I was doing was corroborating the evidence of
the more senior police officer I had been with at the time
of the incident, but I was scared silly that I would say
something wrong and wreck the whole case.'

Slowly she developed the ability to shield herself from
the more unsavoury aspects of the job. The serious crimes
were snatched up by the detectives from CID so, apart
from the initial calls to rapes, child abuse, family squab-
bles or even murder, the more unsavoury aspects were
usually out of her grasp.

As time wore on Hilary found herself with several
changes of companion. Eventually she was told that her

new tutor was to be Ray Sutherland—the division's 'Holy Joe'. With only twenty or so officers on the shift it was almost inevitable she would end up with him at some time. To fun-loving Hilary, who enjoyed the occasional romantic affair provided by Aberdeen's exciting night-life, Ray promised to be a wet blanket. Her colleagues warned her: 'Don't let him convert you,' but grinned knowingly, confident that if anyone did any converting it wouldn't be the dour Ray. Far more likely that the bouncy Hilary Smith would break his religious guard.

Hilary was unimpressed by Ray's sincerity. 'I was ready to show him that he had conjured up God in his imagination to make the inevitability of death and the futility of life easier to bear.'

Ray, however, didn't see the futility of life. And what Hilary had not reckoned on was the confident, calm way he talked about Jesus—as if they were good friends with a personal relationship. Jesus, Ray told her, had changed his life; and the fatherly cop certainly lived up to his preaching. Ray was also sensitive about the right time to speak about religion—he rarely initiated the conversations, but held back until the curious Hilary prodded him into a fresh revelation. Twice she listened as he shared his faith with people they were helping. Called to a home after a family argument that had reached bursting point, Ray had defused the situation and then used his own experience to point out that there had been a time when drink and playing guitar in a band had seemed the only answer to him, before Jesus had been allowed to change his life.

'It all seemed to real, so personal,' she admitted.

As they whiled away the more boring early morning hours of morning patrol—after the pubs had closed and the streets had cleared—Hilary dug further. Ray told her about sin, forgiveness and the cross upon which Jesus Christ had died, the cross which had brought tears from her when she had seen the pictures in her book as a child. As they leaned back in the seats of the patrol car one morning Ray, a kind man, but tough and no 'door mat' as Hilary had observed in their work, likened Christianity to a trial. With eighteen months of police life behind her by now—including plenty of experience in court—Hilary could see the analogy.

'It is as if it is your trial,' Ray said. 'You are accused of being a sinner; God is the judge. The evidence is all against you and your defence can't stand against the list of offences as the judge pronounces sentence.'

Hilary's mind was whirling, recognizing not only the significance of what Ray was saying, but also the feeling in her own heart. She actually did want to be free from the fun-loving yet empty lifestyle she had settled for. The moral influence of her parents produced feelings of guilt that condemned her. She felt the pressure of being in the dock.

Ray continued: 'The judge pronounces sentence—death. It is a just decision because the Bible says that everyone has sinned and that the wages of sin is death. Sin has no place in God's presence.' But as the awful picture he was painting reached its blackest and most depressing point Ray filled it with light: 'Jesus is stepping into the court. He tells the judge that 2,000 years ago he died in your place. It should have been you but he died instead. The judge consults his records to find it is true. You can walk free—Jesus promises you a new life.'

Hilary felt a surge of relief—she never forgot that moment. Ray had previously given her a small booklet, *Journey into Life* by Norman Warren, a booklet she had tucked away in a cupboard in the flat along with the unused New Testament the Gideons had presented her with when they had visited the police college a year before. In the peace of her home Hilary read through the booklet, examined the prayer of commitment at the end, and, kneeling, prayed the prayer. It was a beginning.

It took her two days to raise the courage to tell Ray. He had just steered the patrol car round a roundabout when she took a gulp and burst out with her news. Ray shouted, 'Hallelujah,' and the white police car wobbled as he praised God. He drove out of town to a quiet area within the confines of their beat, drew the vehicle into the road-side, and they prayed a prayer of thankfulness.

If Hilary thought it would bring instant peace, however, she was mistaken. For six months she tried to throw off the shackles of her old life but found it difficult. Invited to a dinner dance with the other members of her shift, she was determined not to be sucked into the social whirl that had previously dragged her down. As they gathered round the bar after the meal she rejected the offered spirits—choosing wine instead. It was a futile gesture, she realized afterwards.

The small house fellowship which she had joined intro-duced her to the power that was to make all the differ-ence. She listened to the members talk of the Holy Spirit and the power he could put into lives and longed for that power. Taken by a friend to a Christian Businessmen's Full Gospel dinner, she responded to the invitation to be prayed for. The power for which she was seeking didn't come. She returned home disappointed. She and her friend talked together—a conversation which reinforced her previous reading about the Holy Spirit—and when they prayed Hilary found herself speaking in tongues. The feeling of strength and comfort that experience gave her encouraged her to face life with Jesus.

At work the glances of the other officers watching for the old Hilary to reappear, became more puzzled. Hilary's faith grew stronger. She was able to tell her parents about the change and, bemused as they were, they attended her baptismal service in a local Baptist church. Coming out of the water, Hilary found tears streaming from her eyes.

She continued to sob throughout the service. It obviously touched her parents.

But the strength that had come into her spiritual life seemed unable to help her in her work. She found herself facing an increasing struggle. She was dropping the shield she had built round her inner self as a necessary protection against the despair she met with every day in her job. Once she found herself crying after locking the cell doors behind a woman. Then came the incident with the man whose daughter had gone missing. She began to feel that her uniform was a barrier between her and the people she now desperately wanted to reach for Christ.

Her dilemma came to a head a year later, towards the end of her third year in the force. Promotion exams loomed but the growing desire to be involved in some form of mission work for God sent her mind into a turmoil. On duty one evening she took her Bible into the rest-room to puzzle things out. 'I knew I wasn't handling things as well in my work as I had been. I really wanted to do something for God.' So she called on God to show her what to do. The Bible fell open and revealed Paul's words to the Romans: 'Those who were not told about him will see, and those who have not heard will understand' (15:21).

Set as poetry in her New International Version of the Bible, this verse stood out from the rest of the text. 'Thank you, Lord,' she breathed—and a split second later began to doubt. But when she discussed it with Ray he pointed out that if she had been asking God for guidance she mustn't doubt when it came.

Two days later she put in her letter of resignation. This letter sparked a chain of interviews—first her Duty Inspector, who, surprised at her action, was anxious to make certain Ray hadn't wrongly influenced her. She assured him it was her decision, and told him of her desire to work for God. The Divisional Commander spoke to her.

A lay-preacher, he surprised her by his final comment: 'Hilary, I'm glad you're not my daughter.' Finally the Assistant Chief Constable faced her and, after listening to her testimony, agreed to accept the resignation.

A couple in her fellowship—The Westhill Christian Fellowship—had previously worked for Operation Mobilisation, a mission organization which specializes in short-term training of young people in direct evangelism. Their work, and the fact that the organization operated in France, interested Hilary and she wrote asking about their continental summer campaigns. It would be something to do while waiting to hear the result of her interview for a place at a teacher-training college.

Accepted by OM for the summer, she travelled to London to join a group of young Christians to discover the techniques of evangelism in another language. She humped her rucksack from Hern Hill station the two miles to a church at which they had been told to assemble. Fifty little children were there with youth leaders—but no OM personnel. They were, she was told, expected. Hilary was the first to arrive.

Over the next few hours about twenty young people gathered in the church, before hiking, with a leader, back to the station on their way to Belgium. After a placid crossing of the channel they were directed on board a train, to alight at Leuven, Belgium, where a battered mini-bus ferried them to an impressive, large Bible school. The spacious grounds gave the building an imposing appearance as around two hundred young people gathered from all over the Continent and North America.

The days that followed blurred with activity. George Verwer, leader and founder of the organization, spoke and challenged the youngsters with the needs of the world. There were Bible studies, seminars on how to adapt to a new country, helpful advice on how to witness and act, and always the challenge of the different countries needing Christian witness.

The walls of the school—even the stairways—were smothered in posters from the European countries to which teams would be sent: France, Belgium, Germany, Spain, Ireland, and Britain. Hilary's choice, France, was confirmed and at the end of the week she squashed into a mini-bus with eight other girls under the direction of Heidi Laumann from Switzerland, given a map, enough money for the journey, boxes of Bibles, New Testaments, tracts and other Christian literature, and told to go to Le Havre. The Mission had begun.

In Le Havre the nine stayed in a large Salvation Army hostel. This meant that, though they were guaranteed breakfast and an evening meal every day, they had to eat under the staring eyes of the dishevelled men who made up the remainder of the hostel guests.

Their work was to go from door to door in the town and villages distributing Christian leaflets and trying to sell literature and speak about Jesus. In the excitement of the Leuven conference it had sounded easy but Hilary discovered to her dismay that selling the Bible was not easy at all. During the whole month she sold nothing. Fortunately, some of the other girls did manage to place the word of God in French homes. Together they prayed for the spiritual state of the people, and also they prayed to God for their daily living expenses, for petrol and food. The girls learned to live by faith, making their needs known only to God.

Hilary shared a room with two Germans, a Norwegian and a Swedish girl. Bible studies had to be conducted in three languages since not all the girls spoke the same languages with proficiency.

As the month in Le Havre neared its climax, Hilary was asked to drive two of the German girls back to their home in Stuttgart. They were nurses who had not been allowed to take the full month's holiday. A proficient driver—she had passed the police advanced test—Hilary drove the faithful old mini-bus to Germany. She collected more young people from the German headquarters of OM in Mosbach and returned to Belgium. The campaign was running for three months—three separate one month periods—and although some volunteers stayed for just one month Hilary was going to be there for all three.

When she arrived at Leuven, however, it was to be asked to lead a team in Dieppe. She agreed. A Christian of only eighteen months, with no sales to her credit in the first month and no experience of leading Bible study groups, Hilary was precipitated into leadership. But God helped the former policewoman, giving different gifts and abilities to the new nine-girl team. Terrified of her responsibilities, Hilary beavered away. The second month was as tough as the first. Living in another Salvation Army-owned building—an old house—they sold little, and ate little.

In July, at the end of the second month, the team were invited to spend a week's holiday with a Christian family. The husband was a butcher and they 'ate like queens'. It was a relaxing and refreshing way to end the month. It also introduced Hilary to the couple who, when she returned to Dieppe to lead a final group for a month, would leave boxes of food for the girls when they returned from their largely abortive attempts to distribute tracts and sell books.

God was doing other things for the group. They learned how to pray. When the indicator on the mini-bus petrol gauge read zero they prayed to get to the nearest garage—and did. On one occasion the vehicle cut out completely on the brow of a hill. They coasted down and when the mini-bus stopped Hilary marched off, petrol can in hand, to search for a garage. But she was called back. The man outside whose house they had stopped had produced a can of petrol—enough to get the girls to the garage where they used their last twenty franks on fuel.

Hilary found, as she attempted to minister in the villages, that the French people had an indifference and suspicion she could not break through. Despite the enormous percentage of people claiming to be Roman Catholic—97%—there seemed an inbuilt hostility to Christianity which she could not understand. But it gave her a growing desire to witness more, and achieve greater things for God in the country which was now burdening her heart.

In the middle of her final month she received the expected letter from the teacher training college in Britain—a rejection. Because she had already been praying about a full year with OM on an extended programme, she took the rejection as God's guidance and signed on to work for a year in France. She was allocated to a small OM team assisting a missionary couple, Gordon Margery and his wife, who needed help in planting a church in Rennes, north-west France. Hilary spent two weeks in Scotland seeing her family and members of her fellowship—the church would help to support her prayerfully and financially during the years—and returned to France.

Their biggest problem was the tension within the group of four girls on the team. Hilary shared a room with Teresa, a Canadian. Ase from Sweden and Dominique from France shared another room. All four had strong personalities—they had all lived alone previously and had independent spirits. Occasionally, as Hilary admitted, 'The atmosphere was so heavy you could have sliced it with a knife.' The hurt and pain that Hilary had known in her non-Christian days in her relationships with men, she now experienced in her friendship with a girl. 'Teresa and I really hurt each other sometimes,' she admitted. The great difference was that she and Teresa were also Christians. With the pain came the happiness of forgiveness and a real love for each other. The tears they shed together helped forge a bond of friendship that still survives.

The year was as tough as those three months in the summer. Door-to-door work, with questionnaires, which it was hoped would lead to Christian conversation, proved difficult. Doors were slammed in their faces—there was complete indifference. Open air meetings—despite the attendance of a dozen or so local Christians from the small church—were just as hard. And the little weekly visits for Bible study made to four women in their homes resulted in only one becoming a Christian—and she moved to Mexico with her husband shortly after doing so.

At the end of the year Hilary applied for a place at another teacher training college, pushing to the back of her mind the growing conviction that God wanted her to stay with OM. If she was to be a missionary, she reasoned, she ought to have a training behind her. Teaching seemed the best. But such was the pressure from that inward voice that almost as soon as she had posted her application form, she regretted it, and sent another letter cancelling the request. She agreed to do another year with OM in Rennes. This time she worked with Ase only—it was the final year OM was to help the pioneer work; the church must stand on its own feet.

The twelve months were little different, and with two years behind her, Hilary decided it was time to quit OM and return to Scotland to be a witness to her own family. She had applied for a post-graduate course in social work in Dundee and was given an interview. Taking five days off from the work in Rennes—in March 1983—she borrowed a car to go to Scotland for the interview and to deliver her personal belongings. She was first interviewed by a man, and then, separately, by a woman. The woman seemed sceptical about Hilary's police career, implying it was the attraction of wearing the uniform which had lured her into the force. The woman also explained the difficulties of being a Christian in social work, a salutory warning to Hilary. 'I was certainly not going to be tactless, but if

Jesus had the answer to life it seemed silly to dismiss it entirely,' she felt.

Still the voice inside her pressed her to continue with OM, although social work appeared to give greater opportunities for helping people. Having taken her luggage home she prepared to return the car to France. She stopped off at the British office of OM in Manchester while a new engine was put in the car and while she was there a phone call came from her father. The letter from the university had arrived, and he wanted to know whether he should open it and read it. As her father's voice spelled out the refusal Hilary realized yet again that a door had been slammed.

Angry and disappointed she stormed into the room in which she was staying, flung herself on the bed, and shouted at God, 'What do you want me to do?' She opened her Bible to read, 'No-one who puts his hand to the plough and looks back is fit for service in the kingdom of God' (Luke 9:62). God's voice inwardly rebuked her: 'Stop running. You are always running away. Accept what I want for you—don't keep looking for alternatives.'

Hilary knew then that she would be staying on with OM. Sharing her feelings in the Manchester office, she was told that as there was a national leadership conference in Birmingham that weekend, and the car had been fixed, she might as well attend before returning to France. At the conference George Verwer reinforced God's word to her heart—preaching on the very words that God had used to halt her flight. When the OM leader called for a commitment from those who wanted long-term service with OM, Hilary stood.

She returned to Rennes to finish off the year and then helped with the three month summer outreach in southeast France. When she talked to Mike Evans, the leader of the work in France, about her decision to commit herself long term to OM, Mike advised her to leave the organization for a time and spend some months at home, getting to know her own church better.

So she returned to Scotland to see her parents and develop fresh understanding with the church who had committed themselves to supporting her in OM. The small house fellowship had now snowballed into a church with fifty members. She spent six months doing door-to-door work, evangelistic outreach, and office work. When she spoke to one man on his doorstep he invited her inside, telling her that she was not the first to talk to him about religion. Bill—Ray's brother—had been to see him a few days before. Back at home, Hilary telephoned Ray—he had since decided to leave the police force and was working with his brother selling and framing oil paintings—and the brothers visited the man again, leading him to the Lord.

Another woman asked Christ to change her life after Hilary had spoken to her and a housewife whom Hilary had occasionally helped by baby sitting, prayed with Hilary—the first person Hilary actually led to Christ. It was an emotional moment.

While she tasted success in evangelism she received a letter from France asking her to return more quickly than she had anticipated as her help was needed. In March 1984 Hilary settled into the French headquarters of OM in Fontenay-sous-Bois, an eastern suburb of Paris. In an elderly house converted into living quarters for the Paris team, and in offices in an adjacent house with a straggling extension, she acts as English secretary to the summer campaign leader in France, Chris Short. She also helps with the missions, and is spiritual adviser to the two dozen or so OM girl volunteers working all over France.

On Friday nights she often joins the team in Paris—boosted to forty people by YWAM and local church volunteers—singing, testifying, and giving out literature on the streets of the French capital. In the shadow of the

stark skeleton-like framework of the George Pompidou
building, and among the roadside cafés, they have their
open-air meetings and Hilary tells the Parisiennes and
tourists about the Saviour who transformed a tough,
Aberdeen cop into a girl whose missionary heart is burning for France and the people of France.

On one occasion a police van stopped near the open air
meeting and Hilary spoke to the two young gendarmes.
French—thanks to her father's careful tuition—falls naturally from her lips. The officers, she discovered, were as
tough in Paris as Aberdeen. But she is convinced that God
will break through. And thirty-year-old Hilary has dedicated herself to working for that end.

6

PAUL SHEPHERD
One of God's Eastenders

The van chugged to a halt outside the semi-detached
house in Mitcham, and Paul and Debbie Shepherd
watched apprehensively as the furniture they had accumu-
lated over the years was carefully eased over the tailboard and into their new home. As they began to shuffle
boxes from one room to the next with the eager enthusiasm of any young couple setting up home Paul reflected
on the amazing turn his life had taken to bring him to that
place.

When Paul was born in Islington, north London, his
father wasn't around—he was probably in prison, having
been caught fraudulently using a stolen cheque book. His
mother was a housewife, frustrated by the demands of
caring, mostly single-handedly, for seven children—of
whom the three boys seemed set to follow their father's
example and discover new ways of breaking the law.

The family lived with a grandmother. Paul recalled: 'I
was born in her bed—in the back bedroom of a three-
bedroomed house. In the front room there was a huge,
battered settee on which we children played. I can't remember where we all slept—only that I slept with my Nan
and a brother.' Playing was what Paul did best, out in the

streets, chasing enthusiastically round an 'Eastenders' setting. His father hardly ever appeared. Even when he was released from prison, he didn't live with the family but instead made occasional visits to see his wife. It was Nan, rather than his parents, who brought Paul up. 'We were very close—I was her favourite.'

When he was four the family moved to Hackney. Nan stayed where she was and Mum took the few precious belongings the family had and loaded them into a car with the children for the ride across London. It was a council flat into which they moved, a three-bedroomed prison in the centre of a very large council estate.

Paul also started school. 'My teacher's name was Mrs Green, a big fat lady whom I detested. I hated school, cried a lot, and it wasn't long before I was playing truant, bunking-off in the afternoons to play with my brother round the flats. Mum was hardly ever around so she didn't notice, or if she did she didn't seem to care. Her main worry was the latest man in her life. My twelve-year-old sister, Lyn, really looked after us. Occasionally Nan would come across for the day on the bus, discover Mum wasn't around and 'tut, tut' before getting us something to eat.

'We weren't in Hackney long before Mum started going steady with one man—a coalman named Bill. He didn't like the fact that there were seven children around all the time so he gave Mum an ultimatum: put the kids in a home and live with me or stay on your own! Mum was heartbroken. I think she did care for us deep down but she wasn't that old and wanted something of a life for herself as well. She talked to my dad about it, asking him if he had any objections to us being put into homes, but he wouldn't hear of it. Instead he spoke to the woman he was living with—a large woman with two children of her own, children which were probably his anyway, and they agreed we kids should go and live with them.

'We moved on Grand National Day. A big black London taxi pulled up in front of the flats and we all piled in, luggage, kids and Dad. It was a fair old squeeze. I managed to grab one of the little pull-down seats with my back to the driver but it didn't prevent me crying throughout the journey from Hackney to Walthamstow. I was even worse when I met Sheila—my new stepmother. She towered above me and looked enormous. It was a rented house with three bedrooms which seemed to have elastic walls as we all crammed in, especially at nights. For us lads it wasn't too bad—the three of us had a room between us. The girls seemed to be scattered all over the place and Dad and Sheila slept downstairs.'

Life ticked on for eighteen months. Paul had hardly started school when they had to move again. His father had not paid the rent so they were put in a council halfway house, a dreadful, squalid place in a block in Highams Park, called Woodlands. They lived on the third floor in one room and shared a toilet and kitchen with all the other families on their floor. Paul detested Woodlands. He was sent to a nearby school but his attendance was short-lived.

Eleven months later the council found the family their own house, a three-bedroomed flat in Walthamstow. 'It was better than the previous place,' Paul said, 'and we lived there for seven years—probably the nearest I came to security in my young life.' Security or not, Paul played truant constantly, hating the very thought of school, lacking confidence and friends because he had moved so often without settling. 'I wasn't learning much at school—not being very quick—and that was another dilemma. I began to slip further behind with my reading, writing and other basic subjects. My age made me a border-line case for the school year so the authorities held me back for a year because I was so slow, but that did nothing for my confidence, nor did the fact that I was now not only the slowest in the class but the oldest.

'The only things I enjoyed doing were playing games. When I moved to Junior School—Mission Grove—one teacher managed to give me a spark of hope, Miss Bredon. I discovered afterwards she was a Christian but at the time all I knew was that she showed me some love and care. She would not only help me with the work I was weak at but also took me, and others, to the cinema and to her own house—a clean, neat home she shared with her mother. It even had a bathroom, something pretty unique in my experience.

'Actually we did have a bath in our house—a massive cast iron structure that Dad had laboriously manhandled into the kitchen but had never bothered to plumb in.' It remained idle—a mute witness to his father's failure as a handiman.

Miss Bredon lavished care upon her class and would read Bible stories to the children—this was Paul's first introduction to God. But as with all things in his life, Miss Bredon's concern was a short-lived interlude. Paul was moved to junior high school. Inside a week he faced his first dilemma: there were a lot of coloured children in the school, something new in his experience, despite living in London, and one of them took an instant dislike to the new boy. 'He claimed I had stolen money from a girl. I hadn't but my profession of innocence didn't carry much weight. From then on the lad was always threatening me and the black boys ganged up on me to make life miserable. Any confidence I had managed to regain at the junior school now dribbled away. The fact that I was never picked for football, nor selected for any of the other sporting activities in the school diary, merely increased the feeling of uselessness. I made friends with one or two lads but life was just a monotonous drag.'

The only excitement on offer was in the local market. Walthamstow High Street had a regular market with stalls straggling either side of the road in a bedlam of noise and confusion. On Saturday afternoons Paul and his brother would wander along the stalls eyeing the cash tills. When the afternoon drew to a close and stallholders began to close for the day they would strike, grabbing a money bag and haring off with their winnings through the narrow, winding streets. Occasionally they went into shops where the proprietors were elderly, and snatched money from the tills. It was easy to trick the more elderly shopkeepers, who were less careful, less suspicious and less quick. But eventually one man discovered what was happening and barred the kids from his shop.

Paul had only been in trouble with the police once, despite the fact that they and his younger brother were old adversaries. And when he did come to their attention it was not for stealing from shops. 'One of my friends lived in a house that adjoined a narrow alleyway which we had to use to get home from school—on the occasions when we went! My brother and I noticed an old bike in the garden shed and my brother nicked it. I was given the job of doing it up. I got new gears and gave it a lick of paint and transformed it overnight, quite proud of my mechanical skills. But someone told the friend and the police visited me. I was sent to court.

'That was a frightening experience—although even at the age of twelve I knew little would happen to me. They wouldn't send me away from home for a first offence. I had two chances before they did that. I was scared though and very nervous. Dad went with me to court—one of his rules; he never let any of the family face the law alone.'

As Paul suspected, he was given only two years' probation for the bike offence—a minor punishment. And it didn't stop him thieving. 'Stealing from shops and stalls was, to me, just like any other kid emptying his own piggy bank.' Soon he was in court again, having been caught out by a shopkeeper who was careful enough to mark his money. Paul pleaded innocence, but he was given three years on probation. Since he was already doing two, it seemed a small enough penalty. But he knew it was the last time he would escape so lightly.

Stealing at least gave Paul an interest in life—there seemed little else for him, particularly at school. His school days were interrupted again in an unlikely manner. One day the front doors of the school were locked since a fierce wind kept blowing them open and had already smashed one window and threatened others. That meant the children had to walk all round the school to leave—too much for Paul and a friend; they clambered through a window. They were seen and reported to the headmaster, a tyrannical sergeant major type who ruled with an iron hand.

'Come here, boy,' he ordered when he saw Paul subsequently. Weakly Paul followed him into his study and remained to be lectured on his irresponsible behaviour and truancy. Having established that he knew the boy, the headmaster came to the episode with the window. He told Paul that the school had subsequently been broken into and thousands of pounds' worth of equipment stolen. 'I believe you let the thieves in,' he accused.

Paul went red with anger and shouted his innocence. But he was not believed.

Paul told his dad, who went rushing off to the school breathing fire, to sort out the headmaster. After a blazing row his father told the Head that his sons wouldn't be going back to the school—and they didn't. For seven months they had an extended holiday while the council tried to decide what to do. Eventually Paul was sent to Beaconsfield School, but by then, tired of being pushed around and determined to be a winner, he latched on to some of the toughest boys in the school and clung to their reputations. 'That earned me something nearer respect but meant I was at school less and less; when I was there I was more trouble than I was worth.'

Paul's reputation moved with him to his final school—William Morris, a senior high school. 'By the time I left school at sixteen I could hardly read or write. I was so bad that when the time came for exams at the end of the year I didn't even bother going to school, knowing I wouldn't be able to read the questions let alone answer them.

'I had progressed from stealing from stalls and shops to bigger things—burglary, sometimes during the day, mostly early evening when people were out. I would climb into their houses through a window and take anything that looked valuable. My dad had a couple of mates who were regularly breaking into houses and I learnt a lot just by listening to them. It was a friend who showed me how to slip the catch on a window with the thin blade of a knife, although Dad said a crowbar was better.'

Colour televisions, jewellery or cash were his favourite items; the televisions and jewellery being easy to turn into cash. Gold was particularly simple to get rid of. Sometimes the adventurous teenager would go to the shops in London's Hatton Garden and sell some of the better items of jewellery. Mostly his takings were bought by a neighbour, a fence who dealt in anything.

By the time Paul was sixteen, he was a pretty expert burglar. He did experience one or two near misses, but managed to escape capture each time. Shortly after one escapade a policeman appeared at the door to take him to the police station where he was fingerprinted for the first time. As the officer rolled Paul's fingers and thumb across the black pad and on to a clean white paper Paul sensed this spelt the end. Sure enough, when he appeared in court the fingerprints had led to another thirty cases being marked down to him.

He went to court a week after leaving school, and was sent to Borstal. From now on offending wasn't going to mean nice chats with a probation officer, but the full might of the law. The worse thing about hearing the judge say the words 'Borstal training' was that there was no way of knowing how long the sentence would be. Borstal lasted anything from six months to two years—it meant he had to behave or he could be shut away for two years.

Even knowing he was going to Borstal didn't prepare him for the shock of leaving the court in a police van and being taken across London to Wormwood Scrubs, the prison from which he would be sent to whatever Borstal might be deemed most suitable. Wormwood Scrubs was an allocation centre and he arrived with a group of lads of varying ages. 'We stood in the reception area and were made to strip down to our underpants. Our clothes were taken away, put in marked bags to be reissued when we got out. I sat around with the couple of dozen or so other lads, mostly naked or in pants, some stepping into the showers which steamed along one side of the area. Then we were all given blue striped shirts and jeans. We were taken for a meal, sitting in rows along a massive table, trying to eat potatoes, beans and sausage that had congealed into an unappetizing mass on the plate. It was a good introduction to the next experience—my first time in a cell.'

Paul stayed at the Scrubs for another five weeks or so, until his destination was settled. But finally the day came when he was collected, along with a few others, ushered into another green police van and driven from the Scrubs' yard, through the heavy doors, into London for a journey that took them east towards Ipswich and Hollesley Bay Borstal. Seeing the city change to country through the van windows was like breathing fresh air but Paul was unable to appreciate the sights; he could think only about his new 'home'.

The Borstal was a series of buildings, four houses plus a final block into which those prisoners who were being prepared for freedom were living. It was something of a target to aim at, first to get into the special block and then to be freed. After the usual allocation of uniform—green shirts and jeans—Paul was put in a house and then told to apply for a job. Scanning the list of possibilities, he decided on painting and decorating with plastering as a second choice. They gave him plastering but it was a useful decision because it was to be the only professional training he had in life—and a profitable one when he eventually needed to earn a living.

Paul said, 'I was fairly happy in Borstal, I had my own room for the first time in my life, a wardrobe, writing desk, and bed, giving it the sort of cosy atmosphere I had always envied in other people's homes. Also I had my own key—a real luxury. Work was fun, I was taken to a huge building made up of rows of walls divided into sections where we were taught to plaster, knocking each attempt off and trying again until we got something approaching a reasonable finish.'

Every week clean clothes were provided and each night after work Paul had a shower before watching television or playing snooker—a game at which he became quite proficient. Except for the lack of freedom, life was pleasant.

Each month the officers voted for the boys they felt should be moved to the 'freedom block' and before long Paul's name appeared on the list. So he moved to the final rehabilitation block, housed in a dormitory—which somehow took the edge off the glimmer of freedom—and settled down for his final few weeks.

Already, however, one change, the most important in Paul's life, had taken place. 'I met another Paul—not an inmate but the young chaplain who worked at the Borstal trying to help offenders. Something about him appealed to me right from the start. I decided to accept his invitation to church and found myself in a modern building, with chairs, and a comfortable atmosphere. Few of the lads sang with any conviction, but he was an interesting speaker.'

But it was another group of helpers—young people from Brixton who visited the Borstal—who really began to plot the change in Paul's life. 'I was coming up to seventeen when they arrived and talked quite openly about Jesus and the difference he had made in their lives. One fellow chatted to a couple of us, and as we sat in the Borstal grounds, he used a scrap of paper to show the sort of transformation he wanted us to experience.

"Look," he said, "there's God on this side of a ravine: you're on the other side. There is nothing that you can do to bridge that gap." He drew little bridges—calling them prayer, church attendance, and good deeds—but always making them fall short of the gulf. "God knew about that gap and sent Jesus to die on the cross to bridge it." He pencilled in another bridge, one that actually reached all the way, and put a name on it: "Jesus".'

Something clicked in Paul's mind and heart. 'Up to then my relationship with God had been the few stories in junior school and occasionally calling to someone I called God when I was in trouble with the law. What he was saying made sense. I was told to pray and ask Jesus into my life. When I returned to the dormitory I knelt by my bed and prayed, asking Jesus to change me, confessing that I had been useless and no good and asking for forgiveness. It seemed right to kneel—I was longing to escape the mess my life had become.'

A transformation had begun. 'I knew there was no future for me outside of God and, fed up with life, I was determined to give him a try.' The home of the chaplain became a regular place of peace after the Sunday evening services when Paul joined a few of the Borstal boys singing and talking. 'Something had happened to me. I didn't really know what it was but I wasn't afraid to talk about it. One evening there was a group in my room mocking me, but even as I blushed bright red, I was still unafraid to talk about Jesus. One lad, in fact, asked me after a few weeks why I didn't get into trouble and was different. I told him about Jesus.'

When Paul left Borstal the chaplain wrote an introduction to a local church, but Paul decided not to take it up, choosing instead a Baptist church nearer his home. 'I told the folk I had been to Borstal and they didn't seem worried, but there was always a gulf between us. I couldn't understand what they were doing and why. Within a few weeks I had stopped going. The desire for a car began to grow and it wasn't long before my faith was forgotten in favour of the old skills I had picked up among the market stalls. I robbed a house, did some plastering work and earned the money for a car. My path looked set once more.'

All the good intentions in Borstal disappeared. By June—five months after his release—he was in trouble with the police again, this time receiving a suspended sentence. In September he was caught once more. Paul appeared in court on December 23 and on Christmas Day was spending his second day in Wormwood Scrubs. He said, 'Perhaps it was that which started me back on the search for God and a new life. I was certainly devastated at being back in the Scrubs.' He was there just a few days before being sent to a Youth Prison in Ashford, Kent— one of about fifty prisoners in the Youth Prison which also doubled as a remand centre for hundreds of others.

The three months he was in Ashford were enough to reinforce his decision never to return. When he was freed he returned home and went back to work for the plastering firm which had given him a job during his last taste of freedom. Based in Leyton, they sent him into central London working on many large office blocks, first as a plasterer's mate and then as a plasterer. In his spare time he worked privately and began to realize that there was money to be made plastering—without the fear of being caught.

Paul was working steadily, had money and began to develop friendships—life was fun. He and his mates were always at discos or drinking. One day, through the flickering lights of a disco Paul suddenly caught sight of Debbie, an attractive girl he had first met while working in a supermarket in Chingford before being sent to Ashford. They had gone out a couple of times but Paul had not been interested. Bold and brash—he now felt he was someone in the world—he strolled up to her.

'Let's dance,' he said with the attitude of someone doing the girl a favour. While Debbie was making up her mind, her friend reminded her of the hurt Paul had caused her before.

Debbie, always her own boss, looked up at Paul and said, 'All right.' Afterwards Paul took her home, first accidentally spilling coffee all over her in a mobile coffee shop. It seemed to be a casual relationship that promised nothing. It was only when Paul was out with another girl that he realized he missed Debbie. He discovered he was in love.

The couple talked about marriage. Although her parents were not keen on an early wedding, as Debbie was only eighteen, wedding plans went ahead. Just ten weeks after that evening at the disco Paul and Debbie were married, breezing through the ceremony in an Anglican church in Chingford. They lived with Debbie's parents while hunting for a flat, Paul earning good money plastering and Debbie working in a bank.

Because Paul could earn more working privately than with a building company he decided to branch out on his own. It was then that his sister's husband, Les—with whom Paul got on well—said he would help occasionally. Les, who was a bus driver, wanted to earn money to get his own house. One Saturday the pair went to work for an Asian friend of Les', tyroloning the outside of the house.

It was a simple job and by late afternoon it was almost finished. Paul was up a ladder cleaning one wall and Les was doing a similar job on another wall. 'Suddenly,' said Paul, 'I heard a scream, followed by a crashing noise and then a clunk which sickened me. I hurtled down my ladder to find Les' body on the floor, blood spattered all over the concrete and the body lifeless. An ambulance was called, and a doctor, but when the doctor came over to me he told me bluntly: 'He's dead.' I could have torn the doctor apart. I had loved Les and was devastated. Nothing had prepared me for this. Tears wouldn't stop flowing.'

Next day Paul walked into a church in Chingford—a Brethren church to which Debbie had gone for years. As a Covenanter she had made some sort of decision to be a Christian years before but had fallen away. Now she returned with Paul as he looked for comfort, tears constantly coming to his eyes, and the vision of Les' body always in front of him. After the meeting on that first Sunday they went to someone's house for a youth meeting. For eighteen months they worshipped there, beginning to discover more about God and yet never seeming to find the relevance of Christianity to them. The leaders were caring, knowing Paul was hurting, and the couple were baptized and involved in a number of evangelistic projects. The first was a Youth for Christ mission lasting seven days entitled, 'Here Comes the Son.' When the appeal was made for counsellors to deal with the youngsters who would make decisions Debbie and Paul volunteered. There was a series of training classes so it didn't matter that they didn't really understand much about being a Christian. While they were at these classes things began to grow clearer. Debbie realized she had to give her life to God, so she did. Paul too, rededicated his life to God completely.

They were never called on to counsel anyone—it was perhaps as well considering the limitations of their faith—

but they did get involved with youth work with the leaders of the team, witnessing in the streets and in coffee bars, talking about what Jesus meant to them. The mission was led by Tony Dann and Pete Gilbert who became close friends. When Paul or Debbie had problems they would phone Pete, who never failed to go and talk and pray with them. He also spent long evenings explaining what it meant to be filled with the Holy Spirit and the importance of understanding the gifts God had given them to enable them to work effectively.

'One evening,' Paul said, 'we had invited Tony and Pete to our front room—by now we had our own rented flat—and the conversation was getting serious. Debbie was giggling, a sure sign she was embarrassed. I was nervous. Pete tried to tell us that there was nothing to be nervous about and as we talked Debbie was filled with the Holy Spirit and suddenly started laughing with the joy and freedom God was giving her. But I was determined not to be manipulated. No one was going to pull the wool over my eyes.

'I told them nothing was happening to me. I hadn't felt a thing. But Pete sensed something far deeper and could see there was a block in my spiritual channels. We knelt on the floor—Pete, Tony, Judy (Tony's wife), Debbie and myself and held hands praying. As we did, Pete started to ask me about personal problems. God revealed to me that the block was the incident with Les. Even though I had cried at the time I had bottled up my emotions. God began to show me that he knew how I felt—it was like watching a video, I saw my brother-in-law at the foot of the shattered ladder, but this time the Lord stood alongside me.

'It brought back the horror of the occasion. On the morning of the accident Les and I had talked about what we would do when we were rich. Les wanted a Rolls Royce car and a house of his own. Just a few hours later he was dead. Jesus began to bring healing to me and take away the horror, replacing it with peaceful acceptance.

'After that, Debbie and I began to grow rapidly in the Lord. Our experiences with Waltham Forest Youth for Christ were stretching us but at home the church didn't seem to be helping so we moved to the Baptist church in Blackhorse Road, Walthamstow, where George Stirrup had been the minister for about a year. There were not many people there but it seemed to offer the right level of teaching and the older folk certainly took us to their hearts. George was a great teacher and I could listen to him for hours. He brought the Bible to life.'

Paul and Debbie talked about starting a youth group, but it took a visit to Spring Harvest, the Christian holiday in North Wales, to give them the courage to make the effort. Paul bought a load of cassettes and began by inviting young people into their home. It was informal—sometimes they would listen to the recordings, or sing, or they occasionally watched television. Since it was 1982 and World Cup year they sometimes even watched one of the games. Although the tapes contained deep teaching, the youngsters didn't seem to mind and it wasn't long before kids from the local estate began to attend. One of these lads suddenly appeared on the doorstep. Debbie answered his knock and as she opened the door he said, 'Do Paul and Debbie live here?'

'I'm Debbie,' she said.

'Do you have a meeting here?' he asked. 'Can I come in?' He did and within a short time had become a Christian.

Paul was discovering that the most important thing in youth work was being willing to spend time building bridges of understanding and friendship. 'I found it remarkably easy to talk about God. My experiences in Borstal and the enthusiasm I had discovered then, suddenly burst out again. When I went to help with a mission

I couldn't understand why some of the team seemed unable to talk about Jesus on the street or in the coffee bars.

'My frustration was now not with the faith we were developing but with my job. We were both earning good salaries. I was sometimes getting £200 a week building and Debbie was earning half that and because Debbie worked in a bank we had the opportunity of a mortgage to be repaid at only 3% interest. That was an enormous temptation; we both wanted our own house. But we also felt drawn to full-time Christian work.'

George had told them, 'If God wants you in full-time work he will show you.' On one occasion after Paul had spoken to George about the feelings he had about evangelism, George had warned him: 'If God wants you to be an evangelist people will be converted through your ministry. Ask God to convert one or two people—as many as you have faith to believe for—in the coffee bar.'

Paul talked with Debbie and challenged her. 'How many can you believe for?'

She thought for a moment and threw the question back at him. 'How many do you believe for?'

Paul said, 'Sixteen!'

She looked stunned. 'You must be joking. I was thinking of two.'

Paul compromised—and settled on two as a more reasonable number. In fact, by the date they had given to the Lord, sixteen youngsters had prayed a prayer of commitment. That seemed adequate confirmation that God wanted them to join Youth for Christ for a year, working with teams in different parts of the country.

As the couple began to work—and get more hungry for God—Paul discovered that the hundreds of times he had played truant from school now weighed heavily against him. 'I couldn't read or write well. I could hardly read the Bible. Youth for Christ sent us an extensive list of books they wanted us to read—but they were beyond me.

Debbie, who loved reading, came to my rescue, spending hours reading out loud. She helped me understand words. I had the Good News Bible on cassette and listened to that for long periods, but even though I had a Good News Bible and a Living Bible both of which were supposed to be easy to understand I had problems. It was a major battle that Debbie and I conquered together. With Debbie's help I can now read and write reasonably well. I still can't stand writing letters, and my spelling is pretty rough, but I get by. It was another lesson in God's goodness in giving Debbie to me.'

A month's YFC training in Norfolk was followed by a spell in Plaistow, London, leading a team of young people in evangelism. The work grew difficult when one of the young men in the team returned home, deciding he couldn't stand being away from his girl-friend any longer. Ten weeks later the team split up. Paul and Debbie were living with her parents when George Stirrup asked YFC if they could work in their own church. They agreed—and although it was not a particularly successful time, they worked hard for a year.

At the end of that time they were both disheartened. Full-time Christian work wasn't what they had expected. They had problems with cross-cultural work among Asians; Christian young people weren't as 'spiritual' as they imagined; and often the churches in which they were based had different expectations from the couple. Even so, they knew that God had called them, so Paul applied for a job as assistant centre worker within YFC, helping at one of the regional centres in England. Much to their disappointment, they were told they needed yet another year's training. Paul said, 'We questioned that extra year. Debbie was pregnant and it would mean moving home every three months or so and we felt our previous year with YFC had been adequate for the position of assistant workers at a centre.'

But they agreed. Five months later they found themselves in Cornwall working with Lindsay Haman, a schools' worker with West Cornwall YFC. They were involved in witness on the streets and in meeting youngsters in schools. It was the latter work that began to excite Paul, although many of the situations he encountered were far from easy. On one occasion he was sitting in the dining room chatting to some girls about heaven and hell. One girl was bursting to ask a question. Finally, egged on by her friends, she tossed out: 'Has my sister gone to heaven?' She explained that her nineteen-year-old sister had been hacked to death by an axe wielded by a boyfriend. As Paul struggled to get his answer the bell went and a dinner lady cleared the hall—the opportunity was lost.

Four months were spent in Cornwall—a fruitful time. Paul learnt a lot about work in schools and began to learn how to handle classroom situations—it was something he had not had to deal with before. One school in particular was a joy to visit. A Christian RE teacher invited him to help a group of about ten drop-out kids: 'It was tremendous to be able to talk openly with them and attempt to rebuild their confidence in themselves by offering God as their friend.'

While they were in Cornwall Debbie gave birth to a beautiful baby girl—Hayley—but the birth brought as much heartache as joy. Hayley had a problem with her left hip and needed to wear a harness for a while. She also had quite a high level of jaundice and was put under a photo-therapy unit in a covered cot, only being allowed out for food. Family and friends were 300 miles away, so they had to lean on God alone for comfort, but he never failed them. After eight weeks Hayley's harness was removed and at nine months she was walking with no sign of hip problems; the jaundice had also gone.

Accommodation—a regular item on their prayer list—

was the next difficulty they faced. They were given three weeks to leave the flat in which they were staying and again appealed to YFC for help. God, who was miraculously to provide living quarters a number of times in the next year or so, sent a speedy answer. The couple were called to Maidstone where an empty manse was allocated to them and Paul was invited to work for a few months with Maidstone YFC. It proved to be a more difficult area than Cornwall with the children not so relaxed and easy to work with as the Cornish youngsters.

Paul found that God was beginning to use him to cast out demons and heal people. 'This is the real gospel,' he felt. 'Suddenly things I had read about in the Bible began to come alive and some of the deep frustrations I had with the churches I had been in contact with were reduced. God became very, very real.'

The spiritual front was progressing well, but then the church told them that it needed its manse. Paul and Debbie were moved to Medway to work with YFC for an initial period of three months and a house was loaned to them by a church in Gillingham, Kent. The house was up for sale and could be needed at any moment—but the homeless couple couldn't refuse. Gillingham, like Walthamstow, had many children facing problems—kids whose families had mostly moved out of London. Paul worked mainly on his own since Medway YFC didn't have a full-time worker but was run by a couple in their spare time. It was difficult for Paul, who had been used to following someone else's directions, suddenly to find himself alone. He was young, inexperienced, and found it hard to discipline his time.

After four months in Gillingham the couple decided to worship in a small mission hall eleven miles from their home. The church, though small, with only forty members, gave them an enormous amount of love and support. 'This was John chapter 15 being lived out,' said Paul. It was fortunate, for the couple were feeling low, suffering from the strain of constantly changing homes and work. 'It was impossible to build bridges with youngsters in such a short time,' said Paul. Also Debbie was now expecting their second child. With these frustrations they began to question whether full-time work was really what God wanted for them. But each time they faced God with the question the same answer came back—'Yes.'

It was at this time that they were invited to visit Pollards Hill Baptist Church, in Mitcham, South London. The church was looking for a full-time youth worker and evangelist to reach youngsters in an area with few facilities for teenagers. Paul and Debbie had seen a letter written some time before by one of the church leaders to Rob White, YFC's National Director, asking whether he could recommend anyone. Even at that stage Debbie had said to Paul that she felt it was a place he would fit in.

When Paul walked around the council estate near the Pollards Hill Church he felt instantly that it was somewhere he could work for God. They prepared to move yet again, and yet again faced problems over accommodation. It was several months before the practical arrangements for the move were completed and towards the end of that time, while they were still negotiating for a house, the church in Gillingham requested access to the house to do structural work before selling it.

At first they panicked, but the Lord worked again. Friends offered to let them stay in a house left empty as the result of the death of a parent some months earlier. They moved in—once more knowing that at any time the house might be sold. The few months they lived there in Gillingham, making the occasional forays to Pollards Hill to inaugurate a youth club and begin to get to know church members, were increasingly frustrating. Their first mortgage was taking time to come through and every step of the way seemed to present a new problem.

Eventually they moved in with another couple—this time in Mitcham, very near to the church. They had, by now, a further addition to the family—Richard had been born six months earlier. Three months after they moved to Mitcham they shifted their furniture again—this time into their own house. The house is at the end of a short road acting as a link between a large council estate—a mixture of old-fashioned high rise flats and fairly modern homes—and the privately owned houses which sweep towards Mitcham. The front room window looks on to the forecourt of a pub, and the rear windows face the back of the local shops. A library and community centre are a stone's throw away. It's ideal.

'The area is teeming with kids, aimlessly looking for meaning in life. They remind me of myself and the years I spent hunting for something to live for, a reason for existence, and I feel desperately keen to show them Jesus. It won't be easy. Many of them are as tough as I was. Some have even bigger records in the local police files than I had. Some are nervous. Others have been put off Christianity by an over-pious approach or the dull worship they have discovered in some church or other.

'But it is a challenge. Debbie, Hayley, Richard and I intend to face that challenge. We want to do something for God—Jesus did everything for us. Whatever we accomplish probably won't be enormous in world terms—but if it changes some lives it's justification enough. We can do nothing else but try.'

7

KEN GNANAKAN

A Vision for India in a Council House in Ruislip

On Good Friday in 1961 Indian journalist Ken Gnanakan decided he would do something different. He would go to church. It was years since he had been, forced into it as a youngster by nominally Christian parents who hardly attended themselves. Perhaps a bit of religion would now be good for the writer who promised to be one of the best reporters in Bangalore.

Ken had grown so out of touch with Christianity since leaving school that he didn't even know where the nearest church was. One of his colleagues gave him an address and Ken ambled round. It was closed. Disappointed, he was on his way back to the office when, with a screech of brakes, a scooter pulled up alongside him and a friend called out, 'Hi, Ken.' The friend was going to practise music with some other young men and Ken agreed to join them. He eased his wiry frame on to the back of the scooter, pushing aside the guitar which hung casually over his friend's shoulder, and rocked backwards as they took off.

In the small Bangalore home they used as a practice-hall the quartet began to enjoy themselves, Ken flicking his fingers skilfully over the guitar strings and joining in the latest Beatles' hits which were rocking India.

'She loves you, Yea, Yea, Yea,' and 'I want to hold your hand,' pumped out from the walls of the house and the other three started to regard Ken with more than a little interest. 'Hey, man, you're good!' they chorused. That praise gave birth to a new Indian group—The Trojans. The Good Friday outing that had gone wrong had a silver lining after all. At twenty-one Ken was on the launch pad for a rise to stardom.

And stardom came, rapidly and with all the promises of a bright future that it gives to those who break into show-business. Up to then Ken's life had been disappointing. Trapped in the wave of rebellion and apathy which captured the minds of many Indian youngsters in the early sixties, he had dropped out of university half-way through his degree course in chemical engineering. But now he was all set to make a fresh start.

In the growing city of Bangalore The Trojans were an overnight success. The local press called them the Bangalore Beatles. They snared other major Indian cities with their slick, modern style and musical prowess. Calcutta fell for the four dusky-skinned lads who added a cultural flavour to their Liverpool idols' music. And Ken was in the forefront, the singer whose golden voice seemed destined for far greater arenas that those his own country offered. Even brighter lights attracted them. For four years Ken bathed in the euphoria of growing fame, loving each minute he faced massive audiences.

The group was invited to Bombay—another stepping stone towards the fulfilment of their dreams. Unlike most Indian pop groups, they were given airline tickets for the journey, a prime pointer to the golden future awaiting them. In Bombay, night clubs and theatres flung open their doors to The Trojans, and when the lights dimmed on stage the four found themselves eating in the best restaurants with the big names from the world of films. The razzamatazz of it all went to Ken's head. He was drinking heavily, living under the false security of drugs, marijuana and hashish, and dancing until all hours . . . all the while questioning his heart.

For deep down he was growing restless, acknowledging to himself, if to no one else, that his life was empty, meaningless. He knew that the pressures of the high-flying world into which he had been catapulted were eroding the moral principles his parents had drummed into him as a child. He was an empty person trying to fill thousands of empty people who came to hear him sing. In the midst of his success he caught glimpses of the skeleton face of a bleak future.

As their performance ended one evening Ken and a friend who was very close to the group wandered wearily to the beach. Lying on the soft sand with the Arabian Sea lapping nearby they talked; for the whole of that balmy, pleasant night the pair chatted. 'For the first time I heard someone talk sense and I responded sensibly,' recalls Ken. It was a discussion that was to be influential in Ken's life. He decided to leave the group, which then split. Biddu, one of the other key men in the Trojans went on to sing with the top names in the world of entertainment, and produced and wrote the music for two Joan Collins films (including *The Stud*). But Ken felt in need of a more radical change of lifestyle.

He flew to Delhi, the one major Indian city to which he had never been, to look for a new future: 'I was determined to turn over a new leaf, stop the drinking, drug-taking and immorality, and hunt for a new life.' But Delhi couldn't provide the brake that Ken sought from his slippery, downward journey. Alcohol and drugs were his intake—dancing, singing and music his outlets. Nights rolled into days as he tried and failed to capture a sense of enjoyment.

One beautiful Sunday morning when the music ended

and Ken decided to return to the aunt with whom he was staying, he found a group of young people in the house. 'There was something clean and nice about them. They were so different to the youngsters I had left minutes before that I couldn't help but notice. They joked, and laughed.' They encouraged Ken to sing, seeming to enjoy his voice, before inviting him to a party the following evening.

'I couldn't wait,' Ken said. 'I had been to parties most evenings for years but suddenly I was waiting for one, eagerly. I wanted to be with them again.' The party was a Youth for Christ gathering. Bright singing was followed by testimonies that began to touch a chord in Ken's memory. Then the group sang an old hymn, 'Blessed Assurance, Jesus is Mine.' Ken thought back to the last time he had sung it—sitting at his father's side years before. When the leader made an appeal Ken committed his life to Jesus Christ. 'I could sense the excitement of a new beginning. I couldn't contain my enthusiasm and told everyone how Jesus had become my Saviour . . . I had been born again.'

It wasn't long before Ken was in a singing group again: this time a Youth for Christ team. Two months after his conversion he was touring India—not by plane now, but in a third-class compartment on an Indian train—singing to the accompaniment of his guitar and telling whoever would listen of the joy that was in his heart. In colleges, schools, on the street, and at public rallies, youngsters responded and became Christians.

The group ended their tour in Calcutta where Ken opted to stay, living in premises adjoining Carey Baptist Church, as a guest of the pastor. The young man from Bangalore, now twenty-five, was taking the first faltering steps in a walk with God that was to lead him deeper into God's love and understanding.

As he woke early one morning Ken heard a voice: 'I will

teach you and instruct you in the way in which you will go.' He took in the brilliant sunshine which streamed through the window of his small room and, seeing no one, sensed that the words were specially addressed to him. Though it was so early, he rushed to a friend and asked what it meant.

The friend pointed to Psalm 32 and said: 'Ken, this is God speaking to you. You just follow him. He is telling you he will lead you.' Ken knew it was a prompting to serve God full time.

For a few months Ken worked as a reporter on a technical magazine and the days flew by until, full of excitement, he joined Youth for Christ and began working as an evangelist, touring India and sharing the discoveries he was making from the Bible. For seven years he ministered over the sub-continent and neighbouring countries, seeing hundreds of youngsters turn to Christ as he used the talents God had given him. He had written a few plays, and songs, and the voice that once entertained thousands was now gently cajoling smaller, but more important, numbers into the kingdom. His gift for writing was helping to produce outreach literature, and his preaching was invariably accompanied by a flood of decisions.

God was to give him another personal assurance a few years later. As Ken enjoyed a youth gathering in his own home he heard a young man read from Joel, 'I will restore to you the years the locusts have eaten.' It was a promise he decided to claim. He was twenty-five years old when he was converted in 1965, with a wasted life behind him. While other young men of his age had found fulfilment, he had been groping in the dark. He sensed God wanted to restore them to him. But how?

He had met Prema, a secretary in the YFC office and they had married and now had a small son, Santosh. With God blessing his work with YFC, life should have been fulfilling at last. Yet, as on the beach in Bombay, Ken sensed a new phase in his life opening up. One day, as Ken, Prema and Santosh were praying, an overwhelming, powerful compulsion came over him—he ought to study the Bible more. 'I knew it was one area I should develop. My handling of the word of God had been superficial.' As that thought came to him it was obviously felt by Prema— a oneness came upon them as they prayed.

So seven years after joining YFC he left them and went to Australia, where he spent two years studying for a diploma in theology. His thirst for study not completely fulfilled, he moved across the world to England, settling down in Ruislip, on the north-west edge of London, to spend two years at London Bible College and a further two years at London University gaining an honours BA and a doctorate in theology and philosophy.

Ken, Prema and Santosh lived, with their small daughter Anupa who was born in Ruislip, in the home of Vera Brown. They had a bedroom in her modest council house in the centre of a 500 home estate. Prema worked as a secretary when she could to augment the slender family budget. By the time Ken was into his first year at London University the enthusiasm and spiritual vitality which had marked his progress earlier in his Christian life were weakening. 'In some ways I was proud. I was going to be a PhD. My life was becoming spiritually dry—I could feel it—and I was getting decidedly uncomfortable preaching in evangelistic services to which I was invited. I dreamed of returning to India as an academic, a professor in a seminary. It seemed so natural—after getting my PhD there was nothing I could think of other than teaching.'

But it was frightening to think of himself as an academic among academics when deep down Ken knew his gifts were those of an evangelist. God had his own plans. As Ken lay relaxing one cold wet morning in May 1977, his haphazard Bible reading led him to the Acts of the Apostles. The words began to come alive as he read them—startling, vibrant with a freshness he had not seen for months. 'I became gripped with excitement. God's early church had vitality and it captivated me.' Page after page sparkled before his eager eyes, and as he tried to finish he could not prevent his hands turning back the pages of the Bible and re-discovering the third chapter. He saw again the story of Peter and John in front of the temple faced by the lame man and heard Peter's words: 'Silver and gold have I none, but such as I have give I unto thee—in the name of Jesus of Nazareth, rise up and walk.'

With vivid clarity he knew what he was to do. He was to return to India to raise up lame men and women. He saw the church in his own country with young people spiritually lame, limping. 'I knew I had to go and strengthen their legs.'

Thoughts and plans dazzled his mind. He grabbed a paper and pencil and, almost as if an unseen mind was dictating the words, began to write. For thirty minutes he scribbled, outlining the way he would tackle the ministry he was convinced God wanted him to start. It would eventually be called ACTS—Agriculture, Crafts, Trades, Studies. It would not just train young people in evangelism—there were other organizations doing that; nor would it merely train them in various trades, again there were groups performing that task; ACTS Institute would do both! He would teach India's young men and women a trade so that they could support themselves by their own efforts, and also give them the skills to evangelize. It was the perfect combination in a country where the poverty level was such that only the larger city churches could support pastors and teachers—and even they struggled in some cases.

Ken called Prema into the room to read the words he had written. As she did so she looked at her husband and told him, 'Ken, this is certainly from the Lord. Let's hand it back to him and ask him to give it to us to fulfil.' In the bedroom of a council house in Ruislip they prayed and ACTS Institute was born.

In the weeks that followed, as Ken continued with his studies, he shared his vision with his close friends—Ray Harrison, in New Zealand, the leader of International Needs, an organization with which Ken was already connected, and Fred Hill, a veteran Christian who had been Ken's prayer partner for years. He wrote also to his father in Bangalore—the father who had recommitted his life to the Lord after hearing of the change in his son's life.

Letters began to come back to Ruislip—and every one was an endorsement of the vision. In the study of the pastor of Ruislip Baptist Church where Ken was a popular member and helper, Arthur Thompson read the vision and was amazed. He said later: 'Most Christians who leave a Third World culture for any length of time, as Ken had, seem to find it difficult to return. Ken was a very gifted man, academically, musically, and as an evangelist. I had imagined he would become a professor at a college, or get a job in a large church in America. But it was amazing, and quite thrilling, to see from the vision that he intended to return to his own country and use his talents in a unique way.'

And Victor Manogarom, Director of the Youth for Christ in India, who had been longing for Ken to return and work with him, understood the vision and encouraged Ken.

As he completed the thesis that was to earn him the PhD Ken also began to plan and sketch out the vision in more detail, determined that the emphasis should be to encourage young men and women, dedicated to God, to work hard: 'Dirty their hands, soil their clothes, and do whatever was necessary to reach the people of India with the gospel.'

The caste system in his country, he reasoned, had bred a nation who believed that ordinary forms of labour and manual work were beneath them: such labour was only for the lower castes. The Hindu caste structure seemed also to set the pattern for Christians. Ken had seen the same attitude spilling over into the churches. But the whole emphasis in the early church was the integration of work, worship and witness. He wanted ACTS Institute to follow that pattern and create a new dimension in Christian concern. He was encouraged by Theodore Williams, a man experienced in mission work in many parts of the world, particularly India, who reacted positively to the plan. 'This is just the right time for something like this,' he told Ken.

It was Theodore who led a greeting party when Ken, Prema and the family arrived back in Bangalore in 1979. 'In all my life of Christian work and ministry I have heard of many visions coming from the west, and westerners bringing their visions with them. This is the first time we have had an Indian coming back to us with a vision for his own people given by God,' Theodore told the crowd. Theodore did something even more practical: he introduced Ken to two Christian men and pointed out that they had a similar vision. A pattern was beginning to form. Ken was equipped to lead on the biblical and evangelistic side—the two men shaking his hand had other gifts. Viji Raju had a commerce degree and, with a couple of partners, had a telephone component factory employing about twenty-five workers. He was ideally qualified to look after much of the business and project side of the institute. Festus Thomas had an engineering degree in electronics and the organizing and teaching skills needed for some of the basic craft training.

There was also Ricky Gnanakan—Ken's brother. The two had always been close, a bond forged even firmer by Ricky's gradual birth as a Christian following the change in his brother. Ricky had been considering his own future while Ken was finishing his training and had come to the conclusion that the manager's position he had achieved with a weight scale company wasn't spiritually satisfying. He was prepared to sacrifice the salary and prospects in favour of joining Ken.

Ricky became vice principal of ACTS. Viji the project manager with a wider responsibility in the International Needs programme, and Festus took on the organization of the vocational training programme and taught the basic electronic crafts. A team was being developed to fulfil the vision—including a medical doctor, nurses, technicians, evangelists, Bible teachers, office workers and many more.

Despite his own love for preaching and the way he is still being used, Ken recognizes that preaching is not a twenty-four-hour-a-day exercise. 'My heart longs to see people touched by the Lord and I wanted to explore all the other components that make up a Christian life—working, worshipping and witnessing.'

Because the institute was to train people in three dimensions—practical crafts, theology and evangelism—the growing team found a major problem. There were funds available for evangelistic work, and enormous funds which could be tapped for social concerns and development, but it was hard to find people who shared their vision for a combination of the two. Financial backing was limited and hard to obtain. 'A lot of people were waiting to see whether I was talking sense or whether it would fizzle out and end in just another run-of-the-mill ministry,' Ken said. They were not, however, discouraged. The Ruislip Baptist Church helped to support them—some members, such as banker Alan Knott, making visits to the Indian campus to offer practical help.

They rented a small brick-built house in what was then the outskirts of the city of Bangalore—the fastest growing city in the world—and began work. The living room became an all-purpose dormitory for the students, workshop, lecture hall, living room, and dining room. An office—and a kitchen—took what remained of the space. Three young men were wanting to join and Ken invited them to sign on immediately—they became the guinea pigs upon which the project was launched.

More applications followed, and Ken recalls, with a grin, how students who had been accepted for ACTS Institute could be seen walking round the streets on their first visit looking for the institute. 'They often walked past it two or three times, not knowing that the little rented building was the very place they wanted. One young man even walked away depressed because it didn't have the grand appearance he anticipated.'

Growth over the following six years was steady—a one-step-at-a-time process rather than sudden flurries of activity. The concept of training young people over a two-year period on basic skills such as carpentry, metalwork and agriculture, combined with evangelism and a thorough grounding in theology has also taken time to be understood and accepted. 'We still sometimes struggle with students who want Bible training only, and others who simply want to learn a trade,' Ken said.

Others, however, have taken the opportunities offered with open hands—men like Peter, who stayed to live in one of the nearby villages where he was working as a student, and now earns his livelihood as an electrician and enjoys the opportunities he gets and creates for evangelism; or Barnabas, who went back to his home town, north of Bangalore, working in the electrical industry, and is active in youth work, developing skills he learnt at the institute.

Some, such as Paul, have settled into traditional ministries—he is now an evangelist in his own right. Noel, who arrived at the centre as a castaway from an organization which didn't know what to do with him, remained to help in the growing centre. Two girls who went to Varanasi, the holy city of the Hindus, opened a school for non-Christians. The institute helped them get their teaching qualifications and watches with interest their expanding activities among Hindu children.

A year or so after the one room had grown into five houses—and Bangalore had grown so rapidly they were on the outskirts no longer—Ken started to look for another site. He found a two-and-a-half acre plot seven miles outside the city. It was dry and barren, with the reddish soil sporting no vegetation but a few eucalyptus trees. But it was what they needed. It was bought and in August 1981 building work began with the help of TEAR Fund, the English Third World relief agency.

Now a complex of buildings includes a two-storey block, housing the students' hostel, library, and staff quarters. An office block, and a girls' dormitory are near-by with a clinic and small chapel. The rural area round the centre is strongly Hindu but the original opposition from different factions has disintegrated as they have seen and felt the love and care flowing from students and staff at the institute. The clinic helps—more than 1,000 local people a month go for attention, many spurning the state clinic in favour of the institute set-up where they know that not only will they receive treatment for their ailments but love and care of a special nature.

And the chapel is packed every Sunday—more than 200 cramming into its brick walls, almost all Hindus who have been converted in the last few years under the ministry of ACTS. It is a congregation so new to the things of God that they are unbound by traditional patterns of worship. One day Ken had to stop preaching while some of the men cast demons out of people possessed. Then a man hobbled in with a leg rotting with gangrene, the team prayed and he was healed. It is an exciting church—perhaps nearer to Acts (the Bible book, that is) than Ken ever dreamed.

The students—there are usually about thirty—spend

one to three years at the centre and their craft training includes practical elements. A trust formed recently wins contracts from local companies so that the students can make items which can be sold to help the institute funds. The long-term intention is that the institute will be self-financing and that students will learn in an actual commercial situation rather than just a classroom.

The students' day begins with prayer and Bible study, to encourage them to develop a daily walk with God; the afternoons are used for craft projects. Evangelism is as important on the course as learning a trade and students go at least once a week into nearby homes and once a month into neighbouring villages to reach others with the message of salvation. In the villages the team sing and preach to young and old—often attracting large crowds. In the early days of the institute the youngsters were often beaten and thrown out of Hindu villages but the constant witness has not only made their ministry welcome but brought many Hindus into a relationship with Christ. It is because of this work that the little chapel on the centre is attracting so many people.

The centre includes a crêche run five days a week by students, and local children are taught reading and writing and given one good meal a day. This is part of a large community health programme extending to a dozen villages where young men and women are being given the basis of health and hygiene: the whole family is involved in the learning process. Success is beginning to come, despite frustrations.

It is all part of the vision. Since it was started six years ago, ACTS has been its own answer to those who wondered whether it would fizzle out. There are still many parts of India to be touched by its influence, but the response they see is encouraging. Students come from all over India—a vast and varied-cultured country. They are urged to return home and use the skills they have developed. With the biblical and evangelistic tools they have learned to wield they can reach hearts and minds in their own communities which would otherwise be cut off from God.

Ken's vision is not just for the centre. He longs to reach the whole of India. 'I don't want ACTS Institute to become a big movement and grow and grow, but I want the whole church in India to catch the same desire for fuller, deeper, wholly Christian training. We need churches and Bible colleges that will not just impart Bible knowledge but train people in wider spheres of activity. Worshipping, working, witnessing is the key. If we could get Christians in India doing that it would have a tremendous impact on a great country with great needs.

'My heart is burdened for India,' continued the evangelist. 'I want to take Jesus into unknown areas—particularly the rural parts of the country. More than 80% of the people in India live in villages—but Christians seem to concentrate on the big cities. Our witness is so weak in these village areas.' That is one of the reasons why the institute team looked outside Bangalore when they wanted to expand the work. It was not solely to find a suitable site, but so that they could carry the work into a rural setting. Ken is convinced that the vision must spill over. 'I believe that is already happening in a small way. Organizations and institutions are beginning to get a sense of the vision and are willing to talk about more than just evangelism. They are beginning to see that there are deeper concerns.'

Ken sees his own future as a motivator—one who is involved in the life of the church in India helping the church and Christians to discover just what they should be doing to make their work and witness relevant in the country. He doesn't want to retreat from his work in the West, seeing that as an important contribution to the growing needs of his own country, but he does thank God for sending him back to his own country.

'Early on God promised to give me back the first twenty-five years of my life, the years the locusts had eaten: he has done so. I have managed to gain the scholastic qualifications I spurned as a young man, and I am able to use my gifts to bring the good news of Jesus to many. It is thoroughly fulfilling.'

His own work falls into two areas—Bible teaching and leading the church in worship. He longs for Indians to escape from the traditional dependence on age-old patterns and orders of service into a 'far more exciting sense of worship'.

'When I came back to India I was shocked to sit in churches where there was no difference between the meeting there and any Sunday morning meeting in the West. I want the kind of freedom of worship among my people where we can accept ourselves as Indians and learn to define and interpret the church in our own country. I don't want churches to become Hinduized or break away from traditions. All I ask for is an Indian understanding of our church.'

Another burden is for a 'full-orbed mission' among churches. 'Somehow mission and evangelism has been defined only in terms of preaching, of verbal proclamation. But we need to be witnessing, worshipping and working, using all our gifts in all their fullness as a witness, not just words alone.

At forty-five, Ken sees that ACTS Institute is growing so strongly and on such a firm foundation that he could eventually become redundant. He will then be free to meet the wider challenge of directing Indian Christians towards the basic principles being lived out on the institute's site. 'I long for two-fold growth in the church in India—deeper in the word and higher in worship. I dream of a church pressing foward to know God himself and not craving after the blessings of God. I see areas in my own life that must be touched before others are touched.

'I want,' he said, 'a clean heart—and dirty hands, to make Christ known in India.'

8

JIM GILCHRIST
Peacemaker on the Streets

In the centre of Otara, a down-town suburb of Auckland, New Zealand, shopkeepers put iron grills on their windows and installed heavy metal roller blinds. They were fighting a losing battle against crime. Even insurance cover was almost impossible as companies refused to cover stores in this high risk area. The criminals were battle-hardened veterans of violence and looting—and some were under ten years of age! In 1983 the police and local authorities were helpless to quash the wave of violence and looting.

Police concern increased after one shop was broken into and a large number of knives and meat cleavers were stolen. Shop-owners were intimidated by gangs of street kids congregating in the town centre. On one Saturday evening two hundred youths bombarded the police with rocks, bottles and cans for three hours until thirty police, including twelve members of the special policing unit, armed with batons and helmets, were called to smash what became known as the Black September riot.

When it was over two police cars had been damaged and the windows in the police station smashed. Shop windows gaped open, the glass shard-sprinkled empty shelves bearing witness to the devastating power of youngsters running amok. It was not until early Sunday morning that the rioters were finally dispersed.

Inside two weeks a call went out to the teenage gang leaders to meet together again: this time in a youth club with Youth for Christ community worker Jim Gilchrist chairing a peace meeting, a meeting which would also be attended by Maori wardens, a police observer and a City councillor.

The gangs responded. Nearly fifty youths, representing eight gangs, attended the meeting. They agreed to bury past differences and work together to clean up the town centre. They decided to patrol the centre looking for trouble-makers and youngsters who should be at home. 'They realize that the public and the police might regard their plans with cynicism but they just want the chance to show what they can do,' Jim told the local newspaper.

Calling the meeting was a brave step for the youth worker to take. It was a high risk venture—but it was typical of Jim Gilchrist that he should put his faith in the very kids who were involved in starting the trouble. 'These kids are not all bad. They are just young people who need a chance,' he said.

Most of the youngsters—many only ten years old—were well-behaved but included troublesome factions. It was the younger children who were mainly responsible for the vandalism. Once the leaders had personally undertaken to see that the town centre remained peaceful, Jim was confident it would work. He appealed to the authorities to give it a chance—and to give it time. 'The success depends on the attitude of the police and public,' he admitted.

Jim took the gang leaders and members away for a weekend camp to cement the truce. It was held at Manga-tangi Marea—a traditional Maori meeting place, and neutral territory. They played, talked and developed a greater understanding of each other—and of the vision

Jim had for the area in which they lived, which was populated by 38,000 people, mostly Maori and Pacific Island people.

A year later the heading in one local newspaper read, 'Businesses praise Otara crime cuts.' Businessmen claimed a marked drop in crime in the area—and praised the work among young people. Local business association president, Mrs June Dawrant, said a 'very bad' burglary situation had been reduced. She said that the spiralling crime rate in previous years had been 'indescribable' but that the turning point had come when Jim called his 'cool it' meeting.

'Before that there had been a small group of kids leading a lot of others on,' said Jim. 'Afterwards there was a small number of kids leading themselves on. It became uncool and unfashionable to be involved with the burglaries, assaults and vandalism.' Something resembling peace came to the town. For Jim it was just one more step along the road to encouraging and helping kids; a task that is his lifestyle.

The sixth child in a family of seven children, Jim had a tough childhood. There were no holidays and he was required to be up early to milk the family's lone cow and in the summer to pick and pack fruit from the small family orchard. His mother was a keen Christian and tried hard to bring up her family but times were hard. New clothes or shoes were something Jim even grew tired of dreaming about. It was to be years before he could buy even an ice cream without feeling he needed to justify the expense. For a time he lived with a Maori family—the Christian mother had thirteen children of her own and fostered another fifteen. 'She taught me many things about love and care, the fact that God is no man's debtor, and that there is no greater thing that you could ever do than love and serve him.'

Jim's personal meeting with Jesus Christ came when he

was fifteen. He had decided to stay at school in the sixth and seventh forms and go on to university. His family were not in favour so he left home and worked during the evenings, weekends and holidays to pay for his education. Out of respect for his mother's Christian principles he behaved as a Christian when among Christians—but privately he was cool, and trendy, and mixing with a gang of tough teenagers.

He said, 'There were seven nights in the week and Mum had seven children; so each night she would spend the evening in prayer for a different child. Every Tuesday night I knew Mum was on her knees praying that I would become a Christian. It stopped me enjoying some of the things I was getting into.' At fifteen Jim went to an Easter camp. During the camp a leader approached him and started to speak. 'Jim, you think you are pretty cool the way you live a double life, don't you?'

'Yes,' replied Jim.

'I want to tell you, you're not cool—you're a real fool. It's about time you got your life right with the Lord.'

When he told his mates about this they proposed a solution: 'We'll beat him up.' But Jim prevented the action. Deep down he knew that the leader was right. That Easter he decided that if God was God he was going to serve him. 'I knew he was real and worth serving with absolutely everything. I knew that I had to commit everything to God—my dreams, my aspirations, my future, whether I would marry, whether I saved money. It all had to be his, even down to what I did with my spare time.'

So Jim became determined to do something useful with his life. He volunteered to help on a camp being run for kids from a local welfare institution near his home in Dunedin. He quickly grew to like some of the lads, who invited him to visit them regularly at the home when the camp was over. His inquiries showed that only family and relatives were allowed to visit the home—and then only on Sunday evenings. Jim wasn't related—and didn't feel he ought to miss the teaching he was getting in his local church. But in his youthful faith he was not discouraged. 'I believed that if God wanted me to do something to help these boys he would open the door for me to do it on a regular basis and not on Sundays.'

He went to see the Director of Social Welfare and was told there was only a 'remote chance' that he would be allowed to visit the home. However, the director took a liking to the keen young Christian and promised to telephone the Principal of the home and recommend that Jim's offer be accepted. Later Jim rang the Principal and asked if he could meet him. At the interview Jim said how much he had enjoyed working with the boys from the home when he was at the camp and wanted to visit them regularly. He explained that the boys had told him they were lonely.

The Principal's reply shook him. 'I am delighted to hear that. We have been looking for someone to come regularly to help with the games and activities on Thursday nights; someone who would be a friend to the boys.' Jim hastily agreed, congratulating himself on his foresight at calling the social services director who had obviously already telephoned. Just then the phone rang, and as the Principal talked Jim realized it was to the director—it was the promised call. 'I knew then that the Holy Spirit was in all this,' said Jim. The Principal was agnostic and made Jim promise never to preach to the boys—but he did agree that if Jim was asked questions he could reply.

Jim's first few weeks were difficult. He joined in the games, but found it awkward to talk to the lads, and was getting despondent. Then a game of Bullrush, or British Bulldog, was announced. A growing army of youngsters had to stop the others from rushing from one side of the field to the other. Jim found he was the last person to make the dash—facing all of the youngsters. But he made it to the other side without being tackled; a miracle in itself. It elevated him in the eyes of the lads and conversation became easier. Often it was about his faith and love for God.

Eventually Jim managed to get others to help with the visiting—including women who visited a nearby girls' home. After that first visit in 1974, the work grew steadily. But a year later Jim began to realize that despite all the work and a growing love for the boys which led to the development of many good relationships, much of what they were doing was doomed to fail because there was no follow-up when the lads left the home. So he decided to start a regular youth club in Dunedin. On the first night no one turned up: the next night only one lad appeared, so the idea was shelved. Perhaps it wasn't the time. But within months the Social Welfare Director had contacted him and suggested he start just such a youth club. They offered to provide money and refer young people who were at risk to him. In January 1976 the first club was launched and slowly and surely began to gain the acceptance of the local lads. Of medium height and average build, Jim sometimes found himself jumping between axe-wielding youths, or lads waving knives as they tried the ultimate in arguments. 'But,' he said, 'I was never touched. Usually the fights stopped straight away—sometimes they fought round me.'

After two years Jim took the lads away for their first summer camp. This was a success, despite the broken-down nature of the beach-side site. The building in which they stayed had been built on wooden piles which were sinking into the sand—sinking towards one corner of the building where the heaviest thing on the house was situated—a large refrigerator. The dining tables collapsed regularly and the wind whistled through the walls. But it was a camp—and it was great fun. It was also a start. With the weekly boys' club and the annual camp Jim's vision for mission had taken off.

The club was run by others while Jim snatched a year off to complete a degree in educational psychology at Auckland University. His tutor warned him that it was impossible to condense the remaining two years of the course into a single twelve months, but Jim felt otherwise. God helped him through the continuous strain of doing the full-time university course, as well as thirty hours' work a week for Youth for Christ, the organization he had joined because they had shared his youth vision. Jim promised the tutor that if the going got too tough he would drop a couple of papers. The going was tough—but he stuck to his timetable and earned the degree. 'I felt God had vindicated my desires,' he said. In fact, he won the university's academic prize—but was unable to collect it because he couldn't afford the fares to the prize-giving.

When he returned to the club as full-time worker it began to expand—a girls' club was added, the two-weekly visitation programmes to the boys and girls homes were continued, and a comprehensive range of programmes for young people was introduced, including an employment programme with the unemployed. But by the end of 1978 not one single person had become a Christian as a result of the club. Jim was discouraged and wanted to quit. Only the encouragement of a close friend, whose parents had worked as missionaries in New Guinea for many years before revival broke out, kept him plugging away.

At a church rally one day a visiting speaker stood to give a word of prophecy. Identifying Jim—whom he had never met before—he said: 'You wonder if the work you are doing is of me, saith the Lord. I want to tell you that not only did I call you but I intend to make this work grow and multiply beyond anything you have ever dreamed of.' Whenever dark days came Jim remembered that word—and he was never to doubt God again.

Within months the teenage lads began turning to the Lord. It was the breakthrough Jim had been waiting for.

And as the work blossomed Youth for Christ began to see it as the way forward that they had been searching and praying for. Elsewhere in New Zealand YFC had been attempting to reach disadvantaged young people. They had been initiating work with youths at risk—particularly those who had been subject to care orders under New Zealand's Welfare System, but with strictly limited success.

Jim had become involved with Dunedin Youth for Christ, running the normal YFC activities in the city—rallies, concerts, and clubs—for large numbers of young people, mainly Christians. But those evangelistic outreaches seemed to attract mainly the middle class and failed to touch the pulse of the hurting youngsters—those with social deprivation and criminal records. As success began to touch Jim's work among the outcasts, Youth for Christ acknowledged his leadership ability in what was a new area by appointing him to head the youth guidance programme throughout New Zealand. That appointment was to enable the prophetic vision to come true not just in Dunedin, but all over New Zealand.

By the middle of 1982, four years after the work had started in Dunedin, there were four youth clubs, an emergency home, job training programme, a work co-operative for unemployed young people, a drop-in centre, a juvenile friends of the court system, music teams, rugby, basketball and netball teams, and leadership training courses. All of the programmes dealt almost solely with young people sent to him by the police and social welfare agencies—usually referred to as being 'at risk'.

Then in 1982, the prophecy he had received was tested in another part of the country—Otara, a government housing estate for 38,000 people on the outskirts of Auckland. He was to work among a group of young people desperately looking for something from life and finding nothing but vandalism and crime, on an estate made up largely of Maori and Pacific Island people, mostly low income families and many broken families.

Jim moved to Otara with his wife, Rona—a Pacific Islander. The couple had first met when Jim was at Auckland University and working with Rona's sister, then engaged. Just for fun Jim asked her one day if she had a sister at home . . . she had. They were married and quickly began to develop a family lifestyle that was off the usual track—they had four children and adopted another three. And to boost the household still further youngsters in need of help were taken in for short and long periods. The Gilchrist house became home to many of the town's deprived young people. The years studying psychology and sociology at Otago and Auckland University not only led Jim to discover that he had been a disadvantaged child— but also laid the foundation for helping others.

When Jim and Rona moved to Otara it was with a great sense that God wanted them there—but they didn't discover what was needed until they walked the streets of the estate and saw the video parlours packed with youngsters, and discos bulging at the seams with kids. They began to realize that it was the children below ten who were often out late at night breaking into shops and homes and causing wanton destruction. Rising unemployment and rapid urbanization and migration from the Pacific Islands had helped create a vacuum in the town for the youngsters and their parents.

One of the Dunedin clubs provided the basic pattern for the work he began in Otara. The Te Hou Ora Club (meaning New Life), and even the Gilchrists' home, were to become a refuge for many youngsters.

A dirty swimming pool, and Kentucky Fried Chicken combined to give the work a successful start. The plastic pool was in the garden of Jim and Rona's home. It looked poor but was the only one in the neighbourhood. The couple hadn't been in the house long before one of the area's notorious gangs—the Flatbush Boys—asked to use the pool. Jim and Rona allowed them in and often provided a big pot of stew afterwards to encourage them to stay while Jim led prayers. Respect for him grew.

The household was poor—Rona took in washing to help provide basic necessities and the children knew they could afford no luxuries. Television adverts for a special summer offer of Kentucky Fried chicken made their mouths water but by the time Rona had managed to scrape together enough cash to afford the meal the offer had gone and the price soared out of their reach. Leaving some of the lads baby-sitting one night Jim and Rona went to a meeting at which he was speaking. They returned to a darkened house. As Jim entered the lounge lights flicked on to illuminate a table spread with Kentucky Fried chicken. The gang lads had decided to provide the meal to celebrate Jim's birthday! 'It was one of the biggest blessings I can remember,' said a misty-eyed Jim.

Two summer camps in January for boys aged between twelve and sixteen proved so successful that the second phase of Operation Otara began: negotiations to open two clubs. It was an instant success—eighty names going on to the membership list before anything had really started.

Jim and Rona's four-bedroomed house in Otara was used for their own family and the occasional youngster who needed help; in fact they now look after anything from three to seventeen needy boys. When they started fostering in 1982 they soon ran out of space for their own family and the extra 'sons'.

The only answer was to extend the home and even there Jim did the unusual—he extended downwards! Originally the plan began with the dream of an extra couple of rooms to give the family a little more privacy but when Jim was told one day that the seven foster kids sleeping in the garage were to be the subject of a Health Department investigation, he got worried. 'I knew that mere alterations wouldn't solve the problems of health and fire standards—we needed a whole new floor. Plans were prepared and Christian businessmen agreed to finance the project. As work started the economic recession hit New Zealand and the financial support dried up. The walls were built but Jim and his family had to reach their home up a ladder through the debris of the half-completed ground floor. There was not enough money for the labourers needed to complete the job.

The public of South Auckland and a commissioning grant from the country's Social Welfare department gave the financial boost needed for professional expertise but not for the labour. The lads whom Jim had helped over the years stepped in. 'Jim, you've done a lot for us. Get a builder to show us what to do and we'll finish the house.' They did, some working for six to eight weeks without pay. With the house completed the pace of life within the Gilchrist household hotted up.

The hiccup caused by the building delay was soon a thing of the past. From providing 100 'guests' with a bed and 200 meals a week at the start of the year, Rona now often cooks forty meals a day—as well as meals for her own family and, however economically she buys, the food bill is usually twice what Jim earns in a week. But the Lord pays the bills. 'Sometimes the cupboards are as bare as Mother Hubbard's,' Jim said. 'When we are reading and praying at tea-time we pray for food. We've been right down—but we've never missed a meal yet.'

His aim is to reunite the children they help with their parents; and transform the kids. It works. One weekend they discovered forty boys sleeping rough under one building. Most were returned to their parents and a few went into foster homes. A strict policy of strong love, strong discipline, and a lot of fun seems to pay off. During the year they enlarged the house, Gavin Maitland—a former Te Hou Ora club product from Dunedin—graduated from Bible college and arrived at the Gilchrist home to act as 'Big Brother' to the boys there, and give valuable assistance to Jim and Rona.

Local high school headmaster Barry Hogan says that Jim has 'defused a powder keg, a revolt on our streets'. Mr Hogan knows the results from first-hand experience. He had one boy at school who was so badly behaved that when he was suspended the staff actually cheered. After the boy came out of prison, YFC took him on and turned him round—a radical change. They discovered he could cook and when the headmaster visited the YFC camp site at Hunua one day this boy gave him his food, handing it over with a polite, 'Good afternoon, Mr Hogan.'

'What Jim Gilchrist and the others in YFC do is tremendous,' he admitted.

Jim takes the kids no one wants and often makes model citizens of them. The kids are taken to camps, talked to, counselled, and put into one of the clubs run in the area. In the club in Otara—over a toyshop in the main street—Jim's office is tucked away at one end while the remainder of the space is used for table tennis, a coffee machine, pool table, and a poster on the wall declaring, 'Smile, Jesus loves you.' The loudspeaker system plays the music of Christian bands as the youngsters sit at tables tucking into bread supplied by the local baker. It has been a place of activity—and none more dramatic than the night Jim called the gang leaders together for his highly publicized and high-voltage peace conference.

Even when vandalism was at its worst in the town the club was free from trouble. 'There's no vandalism and no graffiti,' he said. And he hasn't resorted to steel roller doors for protection.

Hundreds of kids still pass through the club, some just for food and games, but many because they hide enormous needs—drug abuse, incest, alcohol, abuse, joblessness, family problems, homelessness. And there is always something happening. On one occasion a television crew was hard at work filming a documentary when a boy staggered in clutching stab wounds. No sooner was he taken away than a thirteen-year-old drunk sang his way into the building. The drunk had nowhere to go so he lived with Jim and Rona for seven months before making the first visit in years to see his mother.

In a newspaper interview Jim said: 'A boy says, "Why should I do anything for Jesus—what's he done for me?" I tell him, "Who gave you the breath to breathe?" "I dunno if I want to breathe . . . if God was real why should I lose two fathers before I was five?"'

Answers, said Jim, don't come easy . . . but they take the shape of care and love that is heaped upon the youngsters in the club and upon those who are taken into the Gilchrists' home. It is real news to these youngsters that they are going to receive attention, love and respect—things sadly lacking in their lives.

One of the many who found answers was Shayne. Before Jim had left Dunedin he arranged a Christian foster home for Shayne, whose parents had been killed within a fortnight of each other when he was twelve. Academically bright, Shayne had begun well but slipped into bad company and began to stay out late and take marijuana. Jim tried to correct him but Shayne would have none of it—he maintained that he was old enough and intelligent enough to know how far to go. He stole his foster father's new motor cycle, wrecked it and, because he was put into another home without any other punishment, became arrogant. Later Jim discovered that the boy was in a terrible state, pumping drugs into his body with needles, and suffering blackouts. Undercover police smashed a large drug ring arresting eighteen drug users and pushers. Shayne was arrested, but managed to escape. He was never brought to trial, Jim was told, because he had died in a car crash.

Jim was very sad. Despite Shayne's capricious behaviour, Jim had loved him. A year or so later Jim was talking to a young brother of Shayne at the club. 'Shayne said to say "Hello",' the youngster said. Jim gulped and the boy explained that the youngster who had died in the car crash had been a cousin. Shayne had gone to Australia and was living in Sydney under a false name. But the boy refused to pass on Shayne's address.

Months afterwards Jim found himself in Brisbane on business. When his affairs were completed he felt a burden for Shayne and rang the brother. Finally he was given an address. He went to Sydney and discovered Shayne living in a flat with other youths, drugged, and helpless. For three days Jim stayed with his friend, each evening talking him to sleep with words about God.

On the morning he had to return to New Zealand, Shayne was missing. 'I thought he had gone off so as not to see me,' Jim said.

Then the boy returned, carrying Jim's Bible. He had gone off to read it. He said, 'I saw my life flash before me. This book was like a mirror—I'm in a real mess . . . .' Shayne told Jim that he had knelt down and asked Jesus Christ to take over his life. He said that he had already phoned the airport and booked a ticket to return with Jim and give himself up; Jim was worried, knowing that in the prison to which Shayne would be sent were men who had threatened to maim him in revenge. But Shayne would not change his mind.

In New Zealand the Police Superintendant was so impressed with the young man that this was a major factor to his becoming a committed Christian himself, later joining the board of YFC as a director. And the detective on the original case, who had been reassigned to Shayne's trial, agreed: 'This is not the same boy.' He found Shayne a job as a company representative.

The trial began in front of a packed court. Lawyers and

reporters wanted to hear one of the most unusual cases for years. Shayne's new boss spoke for him and the detective told the court that the boy was completely different. Finally the judge declared that although Shayne deserved to go to prison he had taken note of the evidence that it was not the same boy who had been involved in the case. Shayne was fined heavily and given two years' probation. Within a few years he had paid his fine and married a childhood sweetheart. When Jim moved from Dunedin Shayne took over his job and is now running a hostel for boys in Dunedin.

That, Jim says, is not simply justification for the work—it is a demonstration of the ultimate power of God to change the lives of the youngsters in need.

There are now four Te Hou Ora clubs in Otara—all Polynesian—with one of the four specifically for girls, and another four clubs in Oruhuhu Papakura and Manurewa.

Thursdays and Fridays see an outdoor programme for the unemployed with canoeing, abseiling and other activities—plus a devotional talk. Two basketball teams, plus the same number of netball teams, play in the local Christian Sports Association leagues, and outreach teams do drama, dance, singing and have a band for youth rallies, churches and prisons in other parts of the country. This is solid training ground for other YFC workers.

Less than a year after the work started more than fifty youngsters had made decisions for Christ—more than half being street kids. There are often over a hundred young people in discipleship programmes, which are for youngsters who have been Christians for less than a year and are wanting to discover more about the faith. Jim has his own priorities: 'There are many kids we want to contact and they all have great needs. First they need the Lord. Then they need jobs, people to care for them, counselling and often emergency accommodation.'

One of his biggest problems is finding enough helpers.

'People seem to think that Otara kids have two heads,' he said on one occasion. But Jim has never had problems with the kids he has taken in. In fact on one occasion one youngster nearly got beaten up by his mates for accidentally standing on one of Rona's flowers.

Jim has gained the respect of government and church officials in New Zealand. They don't always appreciate his straightforward Christian commitment—but they can't deny what is happening in the clubs and to the young people.

The usual introduction to the work for a youngster in need is the sponsored summer camp where he finds himself power boat racing, motorcycling and enjoying other activities which he would certainly not get the opportunity to enjoy outside the camps. Then he is involved in regular week-night club activities, often with all the smaller clubs from an area—and similar clubs from other areas—joining in. Eel-stealing, and Mini-Olympics are some of the evenings that grab the kids' interest.

Later he may go on the Whaiora, 'extend yourself' outdoor programme which includes a commando course and stress-orientated activities. All the events have a multitude of aims: to restore a confidence and self-esteem; relieve boredom; but mainly to reunite the boys with their families, or, where that is not possible, to find them a suitable foster home.

After five years some of the street youngsters who began with the club as delinquents are ready to take up roles as leaders. All six boys clubs in South Auckland are run by converts of the programme. One nineteen-year-old was referred to the club five years ago. Now he holds down a full-time job and uses his spare time—and a lot of his personal money—to help other street lads at an emergency house.

It's that sort of result that encourages Jim when things get tough—and there are times when, as a lonely leader, he has buried his head in his hands and cried out to God for help. Usually, then, something miraculous turns up.

One of the financial miracles of recent years was in 1984 when the local city council decided it would no longer fund the Otara club drop-in centre. A third of the centre's rent was being provided by the council but they decided to withdraw their support. A deputation from the drop-in centre failed to convince the council of the importance of the work. YFC board member and Police Inspector John Walker described it as 'a sweeping blow to our ongoing programme of providing a much-needed community youth facility'.

The council made their cuts knowing that the town's record of street crime had almost certainly decreased as a result of the clubs' activity. Despite that setback, the centre has stayed open and managed to remain afloat financially. Each morning more youngsters arrive for the distribution of food to those who haven't eaten and the centre stays open all day for pool, table-tennis and other forms of recreation, reading, coffee and tea—and, more importantly, counselling. The staff work on a rota basis helping the youngsters, who often arrive, with various addiction problems—alcohol, drugs or glue-sniffing, defusing fights and preventing burglaries.

Jim's work for God is not restricted to the clubs, to using his home as a half-way house, or to the development of leadership training programmes. He also visits local prisons to help boys and is desperately keen to see the style of work he has developed take root in other countries. He even sees it—with some cultural modifications—as a pattern that could be successful in Britain's inner cities.

He is outspoken when it comes to the question of why the youngsters have reached the state they are in. Films of violence and gang warfare were recommended by Jim as compulsory viewing for a committee inquiring into the street riot. 'If you really want to know how these young people think and where they get their values from, I would encourage you to watch a video before making your report,' said Jim listing some of the video-nasties that he knew had cult followings among the kids. 'These films,' he said, 'are a major influence on teenagers from broken homes who are alienated by society and hurt by life's experiences. They are open to suggestion because they look for heroes and the kind of violence peddled to them is very closely aligned with the way they live. Unfortunately the onus is put on people like me to try and prove that there is a link but I believe the onus should be on the people who make the money from these films to prove there is *no* link.'

Jim doesn't just ram his words down officials' ears without proper research. 'It stands to reason,' he said, 'that if television advertisers value a thirty second slot to influence the public towards their product, a two hour sadistic movie will do the same.'

He strongly condemns the media for making 'celebrities' out of street youths, and is critical of legislators for failing to provide adequate penalties for those who supply liquor, drugs and pornography to youngsters under age. 'The simple fact is that it is worth while for the publicans of New Zealand to serve alcohol to young people,' he said.

But if he finds himself at odds with the country's leaders he is at one with the kids he is trying to help. And he gains a lot of satisfaction from the occasional newspaper heading which sets the record straight. 'A Real Riot,' read one. 'Getting their kicks out of life,' proclaimed another. But for once they weren't headlines about the unruliness of youngsters in Otara. Instead, they were articles explaining that the kids of Jim Gilchrist's Te Hou Ora youth club had invited other youth clubs to join them for a real RIOT—a Ridiculous, Insane, Odd but Terrific fun-day. Two hundred youngsters from Te Hou Oras had the time of their lives throwing eggs, chariot racing, tug-of-war and with games so crazy it was a case of seeing wasn't always believing.

Jim summed it up: 'When you consider that a year or two ago many of these young people were enemies on the street, to see them now having a night of clean, wholesome fun together, is just great.'

When the fun was over a Youth for Christ team told those same youngsters of the life-changing power of Jesus Christ. Watching them respond was a moving experience.

From the first club of twenty-three boys in 1976 the vision has taken off around New Zealand so that now there are forty-two clubs and fourteen different centres; seven drop-in centres; seventeen open homes; four job creation programmes. There are also two hundred young people, converted through the programme, involved in discipleship classes and training. Half of the full-time staff in New Zealand are converts of the work, many originally referred to the clubs by police and social welfare departments. In Otara all the boys clubs are run by former members. And the work is still accelerating.

The prophecy that encouraged Jim at the start of his ministry is being fulfilled—and not just in New Zealand. God is beginning to take the youngsters out of their home country. What excites Jim more than anything is that it is the Otara kids who are in the forefront. It is an estate despised in New Zealand—an overspill area from which little is expected. But it is producing some of the country's finest young Christian workers.

This dynamic twenty-eight-year-old leader concludes: 'These kids are not junk. To see them grow is the encouragement that makes youth work really worth while.'

He is still committed to the principle he learned at fifteen—'If God is God—serve him. I serve him not just because of the enormous fun I sometimes get from it, but from obedience.' It is an obedience for which thousands of New Zealand's kids who once were without hope, have reason to be grateful.

9

JACK NORWOOD
Engineering for the Kingdom

For fifty-three-year-old engineering lecturer Jack Norwood, 1981 brought change. After twenty-five years' lecturing in electrical engineering at Southend College of Technology he felt stale. His spiritual life was going through a time of transition too. The recognition that his hearing wasn't as sharp as it once had been encouraged him to give up his heavy involvement in Sunday School teaching and Boys' Brigade.

He sat in the office of minister Allan Cox and talked it through. 'What shall I replace these involvements with?' was the question he asked.

'If God has encouraged you to give up something—he will lead you to what you should take up,' came the response.

Jack prayed and left it at that. Ever since he had become a Christian at the age of sixteen he had managed to relax and believe God was in control of his destiny. When he left school in Southend he had taken an engineering apprenticeship. This gave him the practical skills his creative, inventive mind needed. In the fifties and sixties engineers were in demand—there was always more work than people—so Jack enjoyed life. He worked for the

Southend Corporation planning the electrical installations on the local airport, sewage works, schools—and even spent a year tackling the electrical problems of lighthouses with Trinity House. Then he moved to a Quaker company which enlarged his skills to include electronics as well as engineering. He helped plan the automatic equipment for Ford's factory at Basildon and for television transmitting stations . . . it was a wide range of challenges that Jack was introduced to.

A growing family and the desire to spend more time at home with Eileen and their three children encouraged him to take up the lecturing work. 'It interested me, it was very satisfying—even though it was demanding,' he said. And all the while he kept looking for fresh challenges. While lecturing he was often asked to look at problems for outside companies. One firm was tired of Middle Eastern customers who refused to take into account the difference between 12 volt and 24 volt batteries when they needed charging. They would attach any battery to the charger— blowing it if the power was wrong. Jack was asked to develop a charger that would cover both batteries, and he did . . . although it amuses him to think that he did it with the aid of a turn-of-the-century Victorian manual on elec- trical engineering which is one of his prized possessions.

He always expected to find solutions to the difficulties presented to him, just as he always expected to get through life's difficulties. With Christian parents Jack's life was closely linked with the church. In the war years he was evacuated to Mansfield in the Midlands but on his return at the end of the war, when he was sixteen, he was converted and baptized. God has always been allowed a say in Jack's quiet, unassuming life. 'It is difficult to talk about spiritual development—you tend to only talk of the highlights. The real story is hard to describe. I don't think the highlights are the important parts—it is the fact that God is always there and constantly helping.' Jack admits that one of his own spiritual highlights was the birth of his first child—'A real time of spiritual stock-taking. That was a big encounter as far as I was concerned.'

Little did he know it, when he sat talking to his minister that day in 1981, but God had brought him to another major turning-point and highlight.

While waiting to see what God wanted him to do at church he decided he would give his professional life a bit more zip by taking a year's sabbatical 'holiday'. The college agreed to keep his job open while he gave twelve months to researching some of the problems in industry. Jack, a thorough planner, had it all mapped out. He would spend the year with a company specializing in generators, working with a team of engineers on a new range. The company wanted to modernize and Jack was keen to help. The work presented a challenge and was ideally suited to renew his zeal for lecturing.

Two months before the sabbatical started, with all the planning complete and Jack well into his preparatory studies, the company told him that because of financial constraints they couldn't afford to use him, after all. The contract was off. Jack was disappointed, but the practical mind that was willing to toy with the frustrations of a new range of generators would not be stilled by this threat to his proposed year's radical change of lifestyle. He had his sabbatical—but instead of industry reaping the benefit, several African villages and towns in Zaïre gained enormously. For Jack—who had already been using his experience and skills to help Baptist missionaries—decided that he would go out himself and install the new chicken incubator he had designed in his spare time for use in the town of Tondo, Zaïre. This suggestion met the agreement of the Baptist Missionary Society much to the relief of John Mellor, the missionary who was to erect the building to house the incubator and then install the machine itself.

Jack's year was arranged. The first month was spent,

not in the African heat, but in Shropshire, researching and refining his ideas at the Harper Adams Agricultural College at Newport. 'It was extremely helpful,' he said. 'I had the country's poultry experts giving their time free and all the facilities of superbly equipped laboratories. It was a very valuable time, I had a number of different ideas for control systems and was able to select the best.'

The preparatory month over, Jack flew to Zaïre—landing at Kinshasa airport to spend a week in that city acclimatizing himself to the life of the country. It was a very different week from his only previous excursion out of England, a holiday in France. The republic of Zaïre is a huge, almost square block of land, astride the equator, following, in the north, the meandering course of the Zaïre River, and slimming into a sliver-width country when it reaches the Atlantic.

'It was quite a culture shock,' he admitted. The people, the way of life, and the country all needed getting used to. But Jack, an easy-going, thoughtful man who has always enjoyed what God has done with him, soon settled down. His week over, he had one task before going to his base: he was to go to Kimpese, 125 miles to the west in lower Zaïre, to collect 100 baby chicks and take them the 300 miles to Tondo.

He leaned back in the passenger seat of a missionary lorry driven by Andrew North, the supply officer. The main road, badly holed through constant use as the main artery to the coast, provided plenty of excitement—if Jack required it. The night-time drive could have ended abruptly as Andrew carefully pulled out to overtake a heavily loaded lorry struggling along, only to discover another lorry heading straight for them—without lights. He accelerated and managed to avoid a collision.

In Kimpese he collected the chicks, complete with cardboard-box carrier, and made for the airport for the flight to Mbandaka, the nearest airport to Tondo. As he settled into his seat on the small aircraft the stewardess tried to make him understand that the chick-filled box should be put in the luggage section. Jack, pleading ignorance of the language, fearful of what might happen to the chicks if the luggage section wasn't pressurized, hugged them tightly to his chest and stayed in his seat. He spent the one and a half hours in the air cuddling the cardboard box and listening to the chirping of the chicks.

When he reached Mbandaka, he found that the man due to meet him had obviously not received the radio message—Jack was alone. But he did discover a Zaïrian who had come to Mbandaka to meet Clevedon Weeks, an American missionary. Jack, charmingly persuasive, managed to get the man to take him along as well. Clevedon made Jack comfortable and although it was late at night when his unexpected visitor arrived, allowed Jack to shift the refrigerator and table to create, with the aid of a blanket, a makeshift incubator for the chicks. The heat from the refrigerator's heat exchanger funnelled into the cardboard box via the table and blanket to keep them chirpy and warm during the cold of the African night.

Next morning it was off to church and then, after lunch, they loaded Clevedon's car with ropes, planks, winches, shovels, a large jack and plenty of tools for the hair-raising primitive 120 kilometre ride to Tondo. The equipment was not needed—but for one frightening minute Jack thought the whole lot might be necessary. A culvert tunnel under the road had been washed away by the power of the water, leaving a jagged gash in the road. Clevedon didn't notice until it was too late and the car leaped the gap as if it were in a television car chase spectacular and landed on the other side without turning over.

At Tondo Jack spent five months helping to construct the incubator building, fashioning the bricks from clay, gravel and a small amount of cement. They were cured in the shade for a couple of weeks before being used to extend the walls of the thirty feet by fifteen feet building. The new incubator was part of a major project to help the people of the village with food. Their local chickens carried very little meat and were not particularly good egg producers. The aim was to introduce Rhode Island Reds into the country and interbreed them with the local variety in an effort to produce chickens that would lay plenty of eggs, be heavier in weight, and yet retain the characteristics of the local chickens—resistance to disease and the ability to scratch and find their own food. 'It was a long-term project but typical of the far-sighted thinking of the agricultural missionaries.'

Jack also took an interest in some of the other problems in the life of the 2,000 inhabitants of the town where missionary workers are trying to help the local people produce better quality seed crops and vegetables. He sat for days watching the villagers use the four water supplies— holes or springs. He observed the way they arrived, whether they walked into the water, what sort of vessel they used to carry the water, and guessed at how much it would hold. From that he calculated how much water the village used on an average day.

He isolated a site in which to dig a well, with the idea of pumping the water to a small water tower before piping it to the lower part of the village. Before leaving England he had talked to officials at the Overseas Development Administration and they had agreed to finance the installation of wind pumps or solar powered pumps with the aim of helping a Third World country—and utilizing British know-how to provide the pumping equipment.

As Jack was in the middle of his project, plotting the final threads of the system, he received the sad news that because of Government cash-cuts under the Thatcher administration the association was unable to provide the financial support. The scheme was dropped. But it gave Jack the idea for water pumps and that was to prove valuable knowledge when he returned to England.

After installing the incubator—capable of looking after 2,000 eggs—he began to examine the water supply of another village, a smaller more primitive place called Ikomotaka. The system appalled him. The village huts were situated on either side of a narrow valley which led downwards to the water source. All the sewage and water waste from the huts flowed down the hill to the centre of the valley where it made its way to the water supply. 'It only needed one person in the village to have some infectious disease and the whole village was in danger,' he said. As he studied the area and the problems, Jack began to devise a scheme for digging wells in areas where the water could not get contaminated. Then, his mind buzzing with even more ideas, he started to consider the toilet facilities.

The problems he was highlighting were to perplex him for months, even years, as on his return to the UK, he set about developing the means to conquer them. One thing he observed was that the Zaïrians were wood-workers— metal was not a commodity they used very much. He resolved to make use of wood as much as possible.

It was a year to make him think. Living in a new land and meeting new people had been an adventure. He made many friends both from among the Zaïrians and with members of the missionary team; friends like Tata Loleka, a Zaïrian leader whom Jack respects and tries to help.

Even some of the set-backs he suffered served only to teach valuable lessons and strengthen his faith. Short of money at one time—the bank balance was in order but the bank was a day's journey away and he lacked time and transport—Jack sold some of his clothes. 'I had brought far too many, only needing shorts and sandals most of the day, with a shirt for special occasions! Too many clothes, or other items—such as watches—worn by 'rich men' could distance me from the people with whom I wanted to be friends. So I sold most of my excess clothing. Two days later my room was burgled. Lying in bed just before dawn I was amused at the thought that there wasn't much left for the thieves to take. Then I remembered my water-testing kit which had been in the cupboard. It had gone. This was a big disappointment. The kit was worth more than all my clothing because of what it meant to the task in Tondo.

'The prayer meeting was to start at 5.45 that morning and I showered and prepared for it with a feeling of frustration bordering on anger. My prayers would have been tinged with complaint except that on the way to the meeting I spotted a scrap of wood under the veranda. Underneath the wood was the water-testing kit. I went to the prayer meeting full of thanksgiving.'

As the year ended Jack made his way back to the airport at Kinshasa where he was to spend the night with a missionary. As he was waiting for his friend at the airport he got into conversation with another missionary, Ron Weeks—the son of Clevedon who had helped him in his first days in the country, twelve months before. Ron had nowhere to stay so Jack invited him to spend the night with his missionary friend. 'It was the least I could do, considering the way his father helped me,' he said.

On the way to the mission in the early morning, however, they fell into the clutches of a couple of local soldiers who halted the car. The three men were sitting in the front seats since the back of the car was loaded with a wooden crate full of medical supplies which Jack was delivering to the mission. Three men in two seats was not allowed—and the soldiers were keen to point that out. It was, they told the missionaries, too late to go to the office to pay their fines. The soldiers had a solution, however: if the missionaries were willing to pay them, they could forget the issue. The principled Baptist missionary refused. The trio were told to wait until the following morning when the judge would hear their case. By this time Jack was getting a little worried—he was due to fly to England soon. He certainly didn't want to be delayed after twelve months away. As the trio talked with their captors another solution arose. The soldiers were keen to get hold of a copy of a new French Bible recently published. Jack and the missionary jumped at the chance. They would return to the mission and bring back a couple of French Bibles. But the soldiers wanted the crate of medical supplies as a guarantee that they would return. Now it was Jack's turn to jib: 'The case had no padlock and it was in my charge. I refused to risk it.' Another impasse.

A solution was found: Jack and the missionary went for the Bibles—leaving Ron Weeks as the guarantor of their return! He was freed when the two returned with the Bibles. 'And he still writes to me!' grinned Jack.

On his return Jack produced a lengthy report giving his assessment of the situation in the areas he had visited—a document which delighted officials of the Baptist Missionary Society were able to act on. And then he sat down to see whether he could be of further help.

Water and toilets were the problems he looked at first. Three pumps were bought and sent out to Zaïre—one working reasonably well and the other two suffering from the problem of getting spare parts. It took a year or so to get the pumps and eighteen months to have them delivered—Jack didn't want to put his new friends through that and then find they couldn't use the pump because they couldn't get parts, so he set about devising a new pump. He visited an open air testing station which was examining water pumps for use in the Third World and, using a mixture of ideas from the models he had seen, designed one with a minimum number of working parts. That was the simple bit—the cleverest part of the new design was in the materials used—wood!

Any fears people might have about a wooden pump

rotting away were allayed by the particular wood Jack chose—Iroko, the product of a tree growing in swamps. This is a very tough wood which has been hardened by constant exposure to water and does not rot. Iroko was used for the small circular parts which form the underground pumping mechanism, with the addition of a small flap of leather to act as a valve. The tough teak-like wood was turned by lathe by craftsmen in Southend and Stafford. The surface part of the pump could be made in Zaïre quite easily by local craftsmen.

Jack wanted to test the pump, so he drilled a hole in the garden of his Southend home. Under four metres of clay he came to a gravel layer and a supply of water, whereupon he installed a test pump.

In 1983 fifteen pumps were sent out—five complete and ten needing the surface parts made. It took eighteen months for them to get to Tondo—another of the problems Jack has discovered since his return. They were delayed for months in Kinshasa awaiting customs clearance.

Other ideas came to him. One of the first was a new-style toilet—based on the established squatting plate popular in African countries. A wooden and then fibreglass mould was made and the squatting plate tested. They were sent out and proved popular in Tondo. The design was developed further in Zimbabwe and it now has its own stack-pipe and fly trap to keep obnoxious smells and flies from the neatly thatched wooden structures round the plate. Missionaries are now asking for further refinements: such as a mini-version for the children.

He is even working on plans for a plank-built canoe. The idea came to him after he had watched a craftsman in Tondo spend ten months burning out the centre of a tree trunk before chipping away until he had fashioned a canoe. With planks one tree could produce a lot more canoes.

It was difficult for Jack to find the time to develop these ideas and fit in a full day's lecturing at the college. He prayed for guidance and asked the college Principal to change his scale, and reduce the hours he worked. An early retirement—which had seemed difficult to arrange—was offered, so Jack, now fifty-eight is enjoying the extra time that his first full year of 'retirement' has to offer. There is little chance that he will stagnate. In the small Belle View Baptist Church in Southend—just a couple of hundred yards from the Southend East railway station—Jack has set up workshop.

When missionary agriculturist Stephen Mantle went to Tondo he asked Jack's advice about tools. Jack suggested that £50 worth should be adequate, if far from ideal. But they discovered that that amount went nowhere. And that's where the idea of renovating tools and sending them to missionaries came in. Jack's not even certain how the idea originated only that when he heard of it it was such a sensible, practical solution that he jumped at it.

A pilot project in the Southend area revealed a mass of tools of all types—gardening, carpentry, mechanical, and bricklaying—that were lying idle in tool sheds. The tools that were collected were renovated as they were needed and shipped out. Now the small workshop at Belle View Baptist Church houses the equipment for renovating the wide range of tools collected from all over the South East of England. A whetstone grinder burbles away unceasingly giving a new edge to an overworked plane blade. Rows of lumber saws hang while the protective coating of paint dries on their handles, the blades gleaming from the cleaning process. Spades stand sentry-like, and on the bench a row of old-style wooden bench planes await new, keen blades. In another long thin room tools nestle floor-to-ceiling waiting to be selected and reworked into mint condition. Huge drawers are laden with chisels, screwdrivers, pliers, and hammers. Long rip saws hang in neat rows from nails on the wall. It's a second-hand tool dealer's dream, and a testimony to the thoroughness of the handful of workers who now help in the day-to-day running of the unit.

John Varrell, of Bexley Heath, one of Jack's invaluable helpers, sorts the tools as they are sent in and helps identify those that are capable of being remodelled and used abroad. Sometimes tools that are not useful to the missionary enterprise are sold in England—and the money goes to the same cause.

In the workshop a sturdy Bench-Mate holds a large wooden chest being made from thick plywood, ready to accept another supply of tools. It will be filled with spades, shovels, hoes, and a wide range of carpentry tools before being carefully packed with hand-knitted clothing for Zaïrian children—not even the packing space is wasted— and ultimately sent to one of the mission stations. On the wall hangs a series of orders, carefully vetted by the Baptist Missionary Society: KIMPESE—25 sickles, 25 hoes, 10 pitchforks, 15 axes, 10 lumber saws, 20 shovels, 10 spades, 5 carpenter's sets. PIMU—6 carpenter's sets. TONDO—2 carpenter's sets, 1 water pump kit. YAKUSU—Land Rover garage kit. BOLOBO—remains of Land Rover garage kit.

Last year Jack sent out fifteen shipments varying from a two-ton trailer to a box of tools. In his small office next to the workshop is all the clutter of a man anxious to give missionaries and African friends every bit of help he can. Electrical gear dots the work-bench—he's now looking at solar panels and wants to perfect a solar system for operating water pumps and incubators and also to operate an incubator to check the cleanliness of water. On the desk is a clutter of boxes—alongside an old record player that could give up its parts for better causes. A battered briefcase hides a multitude of documents—red tape is the one enemy even Jack can't conquer. He did have volunteer help for some time from a man who managed to get rid of the paperwork almost as soon as Jack produced it—but he moved from the district.

Jack works for two half-days a week in the workshop, spends one day in development projects, and uses his home as an office for the mounting paperwork. He gets an enormous amount of help from his wife, Eileen. Though suffering from multiple sclerosis, she encouraged him to go to Africa, writing three letters a week to keep him in touch with the family, and helping with administrative work which Jack couldn't do from a distance. Now she is part-time secretary—and hostess to the numerous visitors to their home.

When Jack reflects upon the events of the past few years it seems to him that his sabbatical in Zaïre did something to finalize a 'sort of missionary call' Jack experienced when he was a young man. 'I had an inner feeling that I should be a missionary. But I worked it out with God's help and discovered that for me it was a case of serving the Lord in this country rather than going abroad. I was twenty-two at the time and began to do youth work—Scouts, Sunday School and later Boys' Brigade. Not all that successfully; it was routine stuff, but I believe God expects that of some of us.' That missionary call of thirty-six years ago is somehow fulfilled now, however, with the knowledge that he is helping and encouraging missionaries to be more effective in their work and creating better conditions for the Zaïrians whom he has come to love.

Sitting in his office, he carefully examines a solar panel—made in Germany—which he used to recharge batteries and provide three hours of free lighting for missionary hospitals each day, and talks of the wooden moulds he made and sent, along with protecting gloves, to a Zaïrian who wanted to make soap for the town.

'I see myself as an initiator,' says Jack, a diffident man, hardly the image of a zealous all-for-God disciple, as he leans back in his chair and lets his spectacles slide a centimetre down his nose. 'Missionary work is a team effort—we all need to play our part. God has blessed me with a knowledge of engineering and it obviously helps. But we need others in our team—like the two unemployed men who help renovate tools; the retired man who stands for hours at the bench cleaning blades and skilfully repairing tools . . . it's a job for a team.'

He also believes that God speaks to us through our circumstances. 'There is a sense in which if something needs to be done and I can do it, that's a calling. If there are circumstances in which there is a need, and I am capable of meeting that need, I have to consider carefully before God whether I am the one to do so. I find I have made my responses to God through circumstances.'

Those circumstances have led to a workshop in a small church in a coastal resort being used to provide valuable help to the Third World. They have led Jack Norwood, a retired lecturer, with a lifetime's experience of engineering, to make conditions in Zaïre more habitable for the Zaïrians and for the missionaries working there.

10

DAVE POPE
Starting Where You Are

The vision for the *Dirty Hands* project came to Dave Pope and Ian Coffey after a visit to India. Dave gives here his own personal background to his call to God's service, and shows how that call was tested in his local area before he was led on to other work further afield.

*   *   *

Thursday evening at 8.00 o'clock and a small terraced house in the back of beyond of the West Midlands accommodated what could only be described as a typical youth group—energy and appetite unlimited, taking advantage of the hospitality of a young married couple utterly devoted to channelling the lives of the surging mass of humanity that sprawled across their threadbare carpet at fortnightly intervals. Threadbare because they had made it so! This was the home to which they gravitated when there was trouble in the air, a concern to be shared, a new girlfriend to be introduced or another plan to be devised as to how best to usher the drum-kit into the church!

'So what are we doing for our holiday this year?'

'Let's take a mini-bus to France . . . .'

'Don't be stupid—we wouldn't all get in and it would cost too much.'

'What about Filey? We could go as a group and book a coach to keep the costs down . . . .'

And so it came to pass that on the second Saturday of the seventh month in the year 1968, a coach full of noisy, boisterous individuals bumbled along the A64.

Motives were mixed, to put it bluntly. The thought of spending a week with 6,000 Christians had considerable turn-off potential for some, whereas the challenge of being let loose in the holiday camp, with new territory and other varieties of the species, had definite adrenalin producing qualities for others. It proved to be a remarkable week.

Have you ever been to a Christian convention on this scale and witnessed the antics of the first few hours among those who are there for all the wrong reasons? Freud would have had a field day, and Desmond Morris would find distinct similarities between the preening of feathers, the emission of noise and the general 'look who I am' found in the animal kingdom, and the behaviour exhibited on such occasions. All the usual things happened and all the old pranks played—Brylcreem (it was 1968) syringed into the top of toothpaste tubes, alarm clocks in biscuit tins under beds, and honey on the loo seats!

But in the midst of all the fun and enthusiasm, God was at work, and on the Thursday evening of that week most of the youth group were attending a Christian service rally in the stadium building. The atmosphere was electric, and God by his Spirit was at work. When the speaker asked for those who were willing to be used by God in any place, at any time, at whatever the cost, the response had to be seen to be believed. A number of the youth group stood, and for one youth man it was to be the first step in obeying God's call to Christian service. How do I know? I was that young man.

Up to that time I had been involved in evangelism. Charity begins at home, so they say, and evangelistic gifts need to be proved and exercised under the guidance and authority of a local fellowship before being let loose across the globe! Supported by the wisdom of my seniors and the encouragement and enthusiasm of my minister and his wife—dear Alan and Mary Fisher—I spoke and sang in venues across the West Midlands. Youth for Christ coffee bars, our own 'Glory Hole' outreach, open-airs in Sutton Coldfield, short of air in the cellar of a local church— wherever the opportunity came to present the gospel. Most of the time it was a team effort. The Alethians were a gospel/folk band that were in great demand and formed the core of my evangelistic ministry. We travelled further afield at weekends, and as people came to know us we were blessed to be widely used. Cliff Richard encouraged us enormously by trusting us to warm up his TEAR Fund audiences for seven years, and other evangelists in our country invited us to share in their ministry. We travelled abroad, including a trip to East Germany—unforgettable, particularly the expression on the faces of the East German checkpoint guards as they looked at 'the coffin' strapped to the car roof, and then, when we opened it up, saw only a string double-bass!

In all these experiences God was speaking to me. I was studying Behavioural Science at Aston University and enjoying the sponsorship of a local engineering company far more than I was enjoying the actual course! There were times when the intricacies of clinical and educational psychology, social philosophy, political science and ergonomics seemed very dull and boring compared to meeting people on the shop floor and helping sort out man/management related problems in my training to be a Personnel Officer. And yet even that paled into insignificance when compared to what I was doing in all of my spare time—

evangelism! God was teaching me a lesson. I had no ink-
ling of where he would eventually place me, and time and
time again he reminded me that he had brought me to
Aston to work, to study and obtain a degree. There were
so many times when I would have gladly left college and
joined a missionary society, but God said 'No', and it was
through the sheer hard work and the discipline of study
routines that God taught me the importance of being responsible to him for today and trusting him for tomorrow.
It was tough, particularly as I'm not a natural student, but
the dividend was ultimately an honours degree and a
training in social and psychological dynamics that proved
to be indispensable.

So how does a Behavioural Scientist, destined for a
lucrative career in personnel management, end up as an
evangelist with, what was then, one of the most significant
missionary societies in our country?

It all started in 1958 when as a child I committed my life
to Christ. It was at the end of a children's mission conducted by Eric Last at a church in my home town that I recognized the need in my life to trust the Lord. I remember the
evening as if it was yesterday. My Christian upbringing
helped, of course, but that night it all came into focus, and
I remember praying in the choir stalls of the church asking
God to come into my life.

Teenage years found me attending the local grammar
school, where I completed my 'O' levels in four years and
entered the sixth form, and that's where it all began to
happen. Being a Christian requires total commitment, and
until that time I had cruised through my formative years
without too much pressure and challenge, but in the cut
and thrust of the sixth form common room I began to
realize that now was the time to sink or swim. I was particularly impressed by the life and witness of a fellow
student who was a very strong Christian—he was popular,
normal, and he also had a very attractive girlfriend! He

was greatly respected and I realized that if I was going to make any impact in the school, then I couldn't run with the hare and hunt with the hounds. But at the same time I thought that I could never be like this guy, who seemed to be very together as a Christian in an alien environment.

It was on another Thursday evening, but this time at Lake Street Methodist Church, that Dr Charles Stern of the Movement for World Evangelisation was speaking about being filled with the Spirit and the need to be totally open to the Lord. He talked about the dilemma of being all things to all men, and that night I saw that God wanted me to be empty before him so that he could fill me with himself. It was a milestone in my walk with the Lord; not a second blessing, because there had been many before and many since, but a sudden realization of the overwhelming love of God and a deep awareness of his renewing power. I believe that it was at that time that God set me on course for all that he has since revealed. If he had given everything for me, then there was nothing too great for me to do for him.

Whenever I have the opportunity of helping people to discover God's will, I always stress that God rarely uses a person outside their own home fellowship and locality until he has used them in the place where they are. I guess it is rather like the apprenticeship system, where you serve and train with a company before spreading your wings. Some of us have the idea that when God calls us into service we need to present ourselves to a missionary society and Thomas Cook's, take a crash course in paddling canoes, and learn to cope with snakes and curry! My renewed commitment was worked out on the anvil of my local church, and it was at this time that I began to be very involved with youth evangelism, organizing evangelistic concerts in the local school, singing in the youth choir and running home Bible studies. I still had no idea of where God would lead me, but I knew that I had to be totally obedient to him in every area of my life and trust him totally.

School days came to an end, and I applied to university to study social sciences, but because I had a year in hand I also applied to a local engineering company for a student apprenticeship with a view to personnel management. Both applications were successful, and on leaving school I began to work with Tube Investments on their training scheme; a year later I started my studies at Aston University. I also lived away from home for a while, but still maintained a high profile in my local fellowship, particularly at weekends, involving myself in lots of Christian activity. I was interested in music, and it was at this time that the Alethians came into existence.

But then came the dilemmas. How easy it is for us to get our priorities wrong, and I suddenly found the course at university getting tougher! That wasn't actually the case; the real problem was my lack of application to my studies because of my extra-curricular activities! 'The Lord has put you in university to honour him in your studies.' That word of exhortation was given to me time and time again.

Once that major lesson had been learned, I applied myself, passed my exams and proceeded into the industrial year for my time out in industry. I worked in Redditch for the first few months, and that was marvellous because I could travel home each evening. Because my study programme was very light I threw myself totally into my evangelistic interests, and great things happened. The band seemed busier than ever, but folk were coming to Christ. I was also developing a relationship with an attractive girl in my home area. She was a gifted musician who was also involved in her local church, so all was going well.

My training officer at Tube Investments called me in one day before Christmas of that year to let me know that he had made arrangements for me to spend the following six months of my training at Stoke-on-Trent, working for

Simplex Electric at Blythe Bridge. My response was far from enthusiastic! I did not relish working in the Potteries, and besides that, my work in the local church was going well. Surely I could carry on in Redditch? God must have made an error of judgement. If I left the area now, it would certainly mean that the youth work would collapse!

God never makes mistakes, and on January 2nd of the following year I journeyed north, livid with my training officer, and very angry with God. Stoke-on-Trent became my home for six months and, despite my initial protests, when I look back at that time I fully recognize God's hand on all that happened. To be really honest, the Lord had to deal with many things in my life. I had thought that I was indispensable to the life and witness of local Christians, and when the youth group actually grew in my absence the first lesson was well and truly learned! I had also become so busy that I was no longer objective about God's plan for my life. I had had no time to meditate, think, pray and read God's word properly—spiritual banquets had degenerated into fast food take-aways, and my frenzied activities had been no substitute. Suddenly I was out of the action, with time on my hands to walk for miles, to think, to pray and to ask the Lord what he wanted of my life. I would not have missed those months for anything —North Staffordshire proved to be a spiritual oasis instead of a desert.

Time to think and time to pray produced spiritual fruit, but perhaps the greatest thing that God taught me was to put him first in everything. My career prospects had become of paramount importance to me. I worked to be a Personnel Director, and indeed that had been promised to me, but God had other plans and I soon realized that he wanted me to abandon my ambition and follow his will. I began to understand what that meant for me, and I let go of all the excuses I had been making: but what about Tube Investments? What about my studies? My degree? My girlfriend? If God wanted it, I decided, I would work full time for him.

Total frustration followed. I clung on to all the right verses, and in sharing my thoughts and feelings with mature Christians I received encouragement, but nothing seemed to be happening. My stand and open commitment at Filey during the Christian Service Rally helped, but why didn't God do something, or send the Archangel Gabriel with a scroll of intent to give me some insight into what was in store? At one stage my minister seemed to be actually advising me to stay out of 'full-time' Christian service until God pushed me into it!

For want of great revelations and appearances in my room, I returned to Aston University for my final year. I was angry with God; so much in fact that I began to attend interviews for jobs and was at the point of pushing any thought of full-time Christian service out of my mind. And then one morning a letter arrived. It was from an organization working predominantly with students, requesting my presence at an informal interview in London. The capital had always fascinated me and, with the prospect of an all expenses paid trip in the offing, I agreed to go. Two weeks later I was offered a job working with students, and that invitation was to be the first of a series of events that led me into full-time Christian service. On the same day that I received a formal invitation from that particular society, a very good friend of mine, the Rev. Tom Walker, approached me at a lunchtime event in Birmingham and asked what I planned to do in the future. 'Ever thought of full-time evangelism?' he enquired.

It was on the following Sunday, at my own church, that two people suggested that before going into industry I should give at least a couple of years to the Lord for Christian service, and over a further two weeks other specific invitations arrived on my doorstep. It was suddenly becoming clearer. All through this time I was asking God to show me specifics and was studying the word more closely, but even at that stage I expected him to reveal to me a great panorama of what the future was all about.

I had previously established a very good relationship with the Movement for World Evangelisation. I had been blessed frequently by the ministry of its evangelists and had worked with the organization on a number of projects, and so I wrote to the General Secretary, who was at that time Ben Peake, to ask for his advice. Again, a trip to London, but this time God seemed to be indicating the way forward, and ultimately it was MWE who wanted me for their ranks as a youth evangelist.

How easy it would have been to have opted out of college! The fourth year at Aston was boring, and once I sensed the opportunity in my nostrils I couldn't wait to get going, but God indicated quite clearly that it was his intention for me to complete my degree course and so it was heads down to the bitter end! But what about Tube Investments and personnel work? A trip to headquarters and a visit with my training officer served to put him clearly in the picture.

'We all go through these enthusiastic stages,' he said, smiling wryly. 'I'm an atheist, so I don't fully understand what you are saying, but if I were you, I would still follow through on the interviews and see what happens.'

Strangely enough, his counsel seemed right and I did continue with interviews, only to find my interest in engineering waning rapidly and my zeal for Christian work growing in leaps and bounds. And then the ultimate seal came. One Sunday lunchtime, my parents told me that when I was a child they had taken me to a meeting in Wolverhampton to hear Oswald Smith, and he had asked if parents were willing to allow their children to enter Christian service to stand to their feet. My parents had stood. What a blessing that they had not told me before, as I certainly would have been tempted to have finished at

Aston sooner than I did! Years later I met Oswald Smith at his church in Toronto and I shall never forget the expression on his face when I shared my testimony before I ministered at People's Church. What a particular thrill that was!

I was in no doubt as to the rightness of joining MWE, and so I went back to my training officer to break the news. 'Sad to see you go, Pope,' he said. 'But promise me one thing. When you've passed through this phase, will you come back to work for us?'

'Sure,' I replied—but that was many moons ago now . . . .

I completed my studies and graduated with honours—praise the Lord! I sometimes think that he should have the letters after his name, because it was only by the grace of God that I achieved what I did. But I have no regrets and I can now see the tremendous usefulness of such a degree, particularly in counselling, in organization and in helping people realize their full potential.

I joined MWE shortly after I graduated and moved straight into a programme of missions and evangelism. It was all so new and rather intimidating, and there were many times when, instead of being excited, I felt useless and full of doubt. What was I doing sharing platforms with some of the best speakers and evangelists in our country? I hadn't been to Bible College, I didn't excel at anything in particular and I lacked wider experience, but God reminded me time and time again that availability was more important than ability.

Unfortunately my commitment to itinerant evangelism precipitated the end of my relationship with my girl-friend—not because she was against my joining MWE, but simply because it would not have worked. That was a difficult time for us both, and to those close to us who, after eighteen months of courtship, really expected that we would get married. It is only in retrospect that we can fully appreciate the rightness of the decision.

That all seems a long time ago now and a great deal has happened. I served the Movement for World Evangelisation for ten years and am deeply grateful and indebted to the Council for all the encouragement and help in establishing my ministry. Then in 1980, the Lord led me on into new pastures: the Saltmine Trust.

I had always wanted to help others discover their potential in Christian service and, all the time I had been serving MWE, I had tried to involve friends and other contacts in a team ministry. On numerous occasions I had put bands together for specific projects but I wanted Saltmine to be more than a musical outfit. I wanted it to be a means of identifying with local churches, of raising evangelistic teams to work alongside fellowships and, above all, a means of reaching people from all walks of life with the gospel.

Saltmine grew rapidly and our horizons broadened as requests for missions were accompanied by requests to help overseas. Eastern Europe, Greece and India have figured significantly in our world outreach and, of course, it was as a result of a visit to India, with Ian Coffey, that the 'Dirty Hands' project came into being. It would be the fulfilment of a dream if, in ten years time, there were people serving the Lord worldwide as a result of our endeavours.

Joys and excitement have been accompanied with grief and pain. Perhaps the most difficult time came in 1983 when I was involved in a very serious road accident. It shook me to the very core of my being. Suddenly, all the thrill and enthusiasm for the work had gone. I spent my time trying to work out what God's purpose could be in all the chaos. I am still wondering, but I do know that without God's help, and the prayers and support of family and friends, I could not have continued. I do not understand why, but through it all I learned more about myself and about the Lord and I am now able to look back at the time as part of God's refining process as he takes me further on in my walk with him.

The more I see the tremendous needs in our world, the more convinced I become of the urgency of the hour. In our mission we have been privileged to see many find faith in Christ—receiving clean hearts, but I long for the day when we see more people getting involved in God's work—soiling their hands. And where are the guys? Why is it that girls offer themselves for service far more readily than the men? Why the imbalance? There are many reasons of course, but I pray for the day when more guys realize that serving the Lord is not tea and cucumber sandwiches under a parasol in Southern India. We've said it before—Jesus wants us to be soldiers not just sunbeams, and some of us men need to flex our physical and spiritual muscles and get involved!

That Christian service rally seems very distant now, but the reality of that commitment is as fresh as if it were yesterday. Any place, any time, whatever the cost—and that still holds true for me now. God is dynamic and always doing new things and I can't afford to trade on the past and dwell on what God has done. I'm excited by what he is doing and what he is going to do if he has my total availability.

It was a wise man who pointed out that the reason for much of the malaise and apathy around today stems from the fact that we have far too many people holding opinions about this, that and the other. Short term or long term service, doctrinal stances, authority structures and so on, ad nauseam. I agree that these issues are important, but people with opinions never changed anything. God uses men and women with convictions, with faith that develops limbs and muscle, faith that takes holy risks, faith that makes use of the ordinary to accomplish the extraordinary, faith that will ultimately bring us face to face with the greatest missionary of all time.

PART THREE

11

Where Do We Go From Here?

by

Doug Barnett

I remember three things about that February Sunday in Kingston, Jamaica. First of all, it was scorching hot. Secondly, the worship and ministry in the morning service had been inspiring and challenging. Thirdly, the direction and purpose of my life was radically altered.

I had become a Christian at a National Young Life Campaign holiday in Eastbourne, some eighteen months previously. Since then I had spent fifteen months in the Royal Navy. It had been a tough but very formative period spiritually and personally. There were moments when I felt that I was a non-swimmer who had been thrown into the deep end of the Pacific Ocean and told to swim. I also discovered that, when that happens, God gives you flippers and enables you to swim.

Now here I was in this fabulous Caribbean Island. At the close of the morning worship I was invited to join a team who were going to take some services in a local hospital. On arrival at that Sanatorium we prayed together and then were formed into teams of two and assigned to our wards. I was paired with the leader, Mr Ashby. This gave me great security and confidence— which I badly needed, as I had never been involved in such an event before.

I heard my heart thumping in top gear as we approached the ward. I went into overdrive as we entered and I realized that it was a 'female only' ward. I was most embarrassed and couldn't understand why. To make matters worse, we positioned ourselves at the far end of the ward. I was glad that I was with an experienced, older Christian. He would obviously control the service and I would only be asked to pray, read the Bible or announce a hymn. I was almost right in my understanding of the programme itself. Mr Ashby said hello and introduced us. He suggested that we all sing a hymn, after which he prayed and then he announced that there was to be a special guest preacher that morning. That really had me puzzled because only two of us had come into the room, not three. 'Still,' I thought, 'the preacher must have slipped quietly in while we were praying.' I looked around to see who it was. Where was he? It was at that moment when I experienced one of those electrifying, never to be forgotten moments. Like when your hand drill hits a power cable or your hammer lands squarely on your thumb. I realized he was telling them about me. Absolute panic swept over me. I tried to tell him that I had never preached in my life before and could not start now.

That was when the second shock wave hit me. He smiled and said, 'There's another ward that I have to visit. You just carry on and I'll be back in twenty minutes.' He went and I was alone, apart from thirty ladies and their beds. My tongue felt as if it had been super-glued to my teeth! After much struggling, I managed to smile and say, 'Hello, I'm a sailor and this is my Bible. And I am very glad to be in hospital with you.' They nearly did themselves further damage as they rocked with laughter. Sweat ran down the back of my neck and it felt as if my brain was trying to escape. At that point, God intervened. I flicked open my Bible and saw before my eyes Romans chapter 1 verse 16. It was underlined in red ink. I read it out, 'I am not ashamed of the gospel, because it is the power of God for the salvation of everyone who believes.'

'I have marked this part of the Bible because it is very special to me,' I began. 'Some months ago I listened to a man tell me what this verse means and as a result I trusted in Jesus as my Lord and Saviour.'

How I went on from there I can only guess but I was still talking when Mr Ashby returned. I closed the meeting down and then joined him. As we walked in silence, back to the car park, the Spirit of God witnessed to my spirit that this had been a God-prepared moment for me. He had brought me to this place to show me how I was to serve him in the future. It seemed as if all my life had been a preparation just for this one moment in time. God had made it quite clear that I was to be a preacher.

Later that day I realized what a very personal and subjective experience that was and that I needed some outside confirmation of my inner feelings. So I resolved to ask God to assure me that I was on the right track as I read the Bible, and to strengthen my inner conviction as I prayed. In addition I asked that God would prepare me for the future during my remaining months in the Navy, teaching me important lessons that would develop personal and spiritual qualities within me. I asked that other Christians who were totally ignorant of my thinking would come to me and suggest or recommend the possibility of my being involved in full-time Christian work. God answered all my requests and here I am telling you about it. I have described the incident in some detail because I wanted to outline the important principles that operate as we discover God's direction for our lives.

Perhaps you are asking, 'How can I discover God's will for my life?' That's the question I will now endeavour to help you answer. But first of all, we must deal with some mistaken ideas about God's will.

God's will is not a maze, it is an open pathway

As a boy I visited the maze at Hampton Court. It is an intricate network of paths surrounded by high hedges. I spent a lot of time frantically running around trying to find the route to the exit. I got very confused and ran into numerous dead ends until I eventually got out with the help of an adult.

God's will is not a bit like that. It is a pathway that has been cleared for us. Have you read about those early pioneers and adventurers? They were courageous men and women who opened up new overland trade routes and sea routes and discovered new continents, countries and cities. Their discoveries opened up pathways for others to travel. God does a similar thing for us. He goes ahead of us by his Spirit, pioneering the route. He works at the other end of the line. He charts our route and guides us along it. He does not hide the map from us. He loves us and desires the best for us and doesn't let us stumble around. Psalm 37:23 tells us that God makes our steps firm. The Bible shows that God has made his pathway clear to his people in a variety of ways.

> God's will was shown to Lot through angels (Genesis 19);
> to Joseph in a dream (Genesis 20:3-7);
> to Moses through a burning bush (Exodus 3:1-12);
> to Israel in a cloud by day and a fire by night (Exodus 40:36-38);
> to Gideon through a wet and then a dry fleece (Judges 6:36-40);
> to Samuel by a spoken word (1 Samuel 3:6-7);
> to Peter in a vision (Acts 10:9-16).

It is not God's plan to confuse us.

It is not a master plan, it is a personal plan

Adolph Hitler had a master plan. He ordered the breeding of a superior race of men and women. They would be produced as the result of scientifically formulated and researched, genetic and biological experiments. God's will is not like that. He is not producing a super race but a special people who will demonstrate his glory in their lives as they live out his unique and very personal will. God's way for you is not the same way, necessarily, for me. God's design is for every believer to be 'conformed to the likeness of his Son' (Romans 8:29). If we are what God wants us to be then we will very soon discover where he wants us to be. God does not drop his plan for our lives into our hands like the postman drops a package through the letter box, complete and entire. His will is made known to us progressively and personally (Psalm 32:8).

It is not an imposed misery, it is an inner joy

I once talked with a young man who really enjoyed communicating the gospel to his friends. He was anxious to discover God's will for his life and said that he knew God's will was not for him to be a preacher, because that's what he enjoyed doing most of all. He really did believe that God never called you to do the things you enjoyed doing. His unspoken view of the will of God was that it was an imposed misery and not a delight. The conclusion that can be drawn from that idea is simple. It must be God's intention to ensure for us all to be busily engaged in activities that we dislike. What nonsense. God wants us to desire to do his will and to delight in his will (Psalm 40:8).

Having outlined what God's will is not, let us examine some of the areas that we ought to take into account when we are seeking to do God's will.

The inner conviction of the Holy Spirit

Our guidance so often begins with an irresistible compulsion to move in a certain direction to take a particular course of action. The words of Leslie and Bernice Flynn are helpful here:

> How does the Spirit guide us? Often by an impelling word by affecting our mental processes. By putting impressions into our thinking. By energising our minds toward some task. By stressing the urgency of some course of action. By pointing to some need. By jogging our memories. By stirring our imaginations. The compelling, insistent desire to follow a certain course, may well be the Spirit's voice within. Nehemiah said 'My God put it into my heart to assemble the nobles' (Nehemiah 7:5).
>
> Sometimes the inner call is so insistent that it seems like a real voice. [*God's Will You Can Know It,* Victor Books, page 34.]

In Elijah's case, God's direction came through the still small voice—(1 Kings 19:11-18). The Old Testament prophets spoke of having 'an oracle' or 'burden' from the Lord (Nahum 1:1; Habakkuk 1:1). Philip was led by the Spirit to the desert road to speak to an Ethiopian in the service of Queen Candace (Acts 8:29).

But John Wesley's word of caution is important here:

> Do not hastily ascribe things to God. Do not easily suppose dreams, voices, impressions, visions or revelations to be from God. They may be from Him, they may be from nature, they may be from the devil. Therefore, believe not every spirit but try the spirits, whether they be from God.

But how can we be sure that our inner voice is from God? By asking one or two simple questions.

Is what I am hearing and sensing in agreement with the Bible and its teaching? Anything that runs in opposition to the plain and clear teaching of Scripture is not from the Holy Spirit. He does not contradict the word that he inspired. He won't tell you to lie, cheat, steal, commit adultery, or blaspheme, because that runs in direct opposition to the Bible's commands.

Is it weird, peculiar or bizarre in what it says? God is a God of order and reason. The Holy Spirit may use eccentrics but he does not create them.

Is it steadily and consistently the same? Our emotions change and feelings alter, but the voice of God's Spirit remains consistent.

Is it finding outside confirmation? Does the ministry that I am receiving and the advice of my pastoral leaders confirm outwardly those inward impressions that I am gaining?

If you can answer yes to these questions then you are certainly moving in the right direction.

Reading the Bible

When I bought my car the dealer gave me the keys to the vehicle, plus my car owner's handbook. In it were easy to understand instructions about how to get the car to start, how to drive it in such a way as to get the best out of the machine, and how to keep it in good working order. There were also helpful suggestions about what to do and who to contact if something went wrong. I realized I needed to familiarize myself with this handbook. I studied it very carefully and still do.

Similarly the Bible is our 'life' handbook, written by our creator God and given to us for our help (2 Timothy 3:16-17). What an important volume it is. It gives us our operating instructions to help us keep our lives in good working order. It shows how to get the maximum mileage out of a tank full of life. It tells us what to do in the event of a life breakdown or blowout. It underlines the importance of the oil of the Spirit. It reminds us that in a special way our Maker directs our life's journey. So it is essential to read it regularly, systematically, carefully and prayerfully. We discover what God is saying to us through a Bible verse, passage, example or warning. God's word to us is best discovered in our normal daily devotional or study times. This is much more reassuring and far more satisfactory than using the Bible as a 'lucky verse dip'. I have never yet met a housewife who used that method with her 'rare and exotic dishes' recipe book to solve the problem of 'What shall I get my husband for dinner tonight?' Can you see his face when she serves up rhinoceros chops and sauté python pieces?

Read your Bible regularly and, in that on-going discipline, you will discover that the Spirit will impress verses or truths upon you. They will fall into a pattern of direction that is coming from God. This will be underlined by the teaching you hear in church or by a passage brought to your attention by a friend. Alone, the various parts may not seem too important or very significant, but together they have an authority that will strengthen and confirm that sense of inward leading.

This is certainly my own testimony. I had known for a while that God had called me to serve him. Common sense told me I would have to get some basic training at a Bible college because I was painfully aware of the fact that I needed a lot of 'theological flesh' put on my 'experience bones'. That meant I would have to resign from my job as an insurance broker in the Underwriting room at Lloyds. But when? The answer came to me one morning as I was reading Luke 5:1-11. The last verse stood up out of the book and hit me right between the mind and the will. It read, 'So they pulled their boats on shore, left everything and followed him.' Some two years previously my ship had docked when I completed my time in the Service. Since then I had been setting things right in my business life. For months the Scriptures had been urging me to get ready to go. Now the final word came. I felt a mixture of emotions that ranged between ecstatic delight and utter terror. A thousand questions raced through my brain: 'What will my parents say?' 'How will my colleagues react?' 'Have I understood the passage correctly?' 'How do I explain it to the boss? He's sceptical enough about religion. He'll think I'm a candidate for the funny farm if I tell him God has spoken to me.' The questions flowed, but I was aware of a real inward serenity and God gave me all the help I needed to tell people about my decision. It is important to underline that I did not act on one isolated sentence or verse. That God-given word pressed the lift-off button in my life, but it came to someone who was ready to go and at the end of a reasonable count-down period.

Let the Bible be your guide, and along with the inner conviction of the Spirit you will have two strong pointers in the right direction.

Prayer and patience

Travelling along a country road I came upon a restricted traffic flow controlled by traffic lights. The board that was placed a few yards in front of the lights read, 'When the red light shows wait here.' To have rushed past it would have been very convenient for me but utterly stupid. It would have placed my life and the lives of others in risk. Waiting was what was demanded.

Patience and prayer plus patient prayer are essential in our journey along the road of God's will. It is very foolish to rush headlong into important decisions about a career, a college course, marriage and Christian service. 'It is dangerous and sinful to rush into the unknown' (Proverbs 19:2, Living Bible). George Müller's advice reinforces Solomon's: 'Never be in a hurry in deciding questions of great importance.' God is never in a hurry, so why should we be? Sadly we are 'now' people who label everything 'for immediate attention'. We want quick answers, swift solutions and everything tied and buttoned up rapidly. God works to a different time scale from us. His delays are not an evidence that he is not interested. Nor are they his way of preparing us for the disappointment of a divine refusal. Naturally there are circumstances and events that demand rapid and decisive action, but wherever and whenever it is possible, waiting is wiser: 'I waited patiently for the Lord, he turned to me and heard my cry' (Psalm 40:1). Abraham waited years for his promised son. Joseph waited years in prison before he was raised to the position of the second most powerful man in the land of Egypt.

Perhaps at this moment you feel that everything is dark and unclear. Whatever you do, don't panic. My father always told me, 'Son, never get out of a train when it has stopped in a tunnel.' That's wisdom. Wait until the situation is clear before you act. Nothing is too hard for God. There are no prayers too hard for him to answer. Abraham sent his servant Eleazar to find a wife for Isaac. Every man knows it is hard enough finding a wife for yourself, let alone for someone else. What questions must have tumbled through Eleazar's brain! Did Isaac like tall or short women? Would he prefer a slim or plump lady? Would he enjoy a talkative or quiet wife? Should she have brown or black eyes? Eleazar had no idea which answers were the correct ones. So he took his problem to God (Genesis 24:12). God moved in to Eleazar's situation and answered his prayer.

As you seek to discover God's will, recognize the importance of prayer. Find a place where you can be alone, in the office or factory before everyone else has arrived or in the bathroom or in your bedroom or even in your car. Don't waste time getting yourself too comfortable. Use the time you have to pray. Be specific, but don't do all the talking. Cultivate the art of being still and listening. Our noisy world has lost the ability to be quiet. Quietness is your friend, not your enemy. As you listen, God's wisdom will be communicated to you through Scripture or by an inward peace given by the Spirit concerning a particular course of action you have decided to take. It may arrive as counsel from a friend. But certainly, whatever you do, 'Be still, and know that I am God' (Psalm 46:10).

When you have a pressing issue to sort out, the world advises, 'Hurry.'

God says, 'Wait.'

The world says, 'Don't just sit there, do something.'

God says, 'Don't just do something, sit there.'

We run around seeking the counsel of respected wiser Christians and end up all hot and bothered when their advice doesn't concur with our desires. The result is anxiety, confusion and even stress. Consult with God first and let him speak his wisdom into your life. Then you will know exactly what to do and you will have a peace about doing it.

Using your intelligence

Dawson Trotman, Founder of the Navigators, used to say, 'The Lord gave you a lot of leading when he gave you a brain.' Though some of our choices may require supernatural direction, God expects us to use our brain power and thought processes. [Leslie and Bernice Flynn.]

We have been created in the image and likeness of God (Genesis 1:26). Obviously that is not a physical likeness because God is Spirit. But lack of bodily form does not mean lack of personality. So we have the capacity for rational, intelligent thought and moral activity. God's will involves us in making sensible decisions at a human level. The gift of common sense is a valuable one.

We do not normally seek special guidance about getting up in the morning. Neither do we agonize spiritually in prayer about what clothes to wear or even if we should wear any clothes at all. None of us needs a divine revelation to convince us that food is a necessity. We eat or die. We know the importance of wearing clothes, getting up in the morning, eating and taking care of ourselves. These are all activities that involve us in the use of our God-given intelligence. You won't discover a Bible verse that will select the colour of your shirt or tie for you, nor a verse that will tell you what dress and matching accessories to wear each day. The Lord Jesus not only redeemed our hearts, but our brains as well. Jesus told us to love God with all our mind (Matthew 22:37). Paul reminds us in Romans that we are to be 'transformed by the renewing of your mind' (12:2) and urges that 'each one should be fully convinced in his own mind' (14:5). Paul used his judgement when he discovered his life was in danger and altered his travel plans accordingly (Acts 20:3).

Naturally the process of decision making needs some guidelines.

We need to decide what the issue is that has to be decided.

Are we looking for a career or short-term missionary service? We need to be certain in our minds what it is we believe God is calling us to do. You cannot be guided on facts that do not exist. In Ephesians 5:17 Paul urges that we understand the will of God. Leslie Flynn suggests that the verb 'understand' has the idea of 'bringing together', sorting out the facts to enable a good decision to be reached.

List all the possible solutions

Are medical, theological, educational or technical qualifications needed? Do I need special training in any other areas?

Think things through and delete all the impractical solutions from the possibles list

For example, those that are contrary to Scripture or the spirit of biblical truth. If you do not have sufficient cash for the training you think you require, it is not God's leading to fiddle your tax return in order to raise that support.

Assess prayerfully and carefully what remains

It may be that engineers are needed to sink a waterhole and help with the development of a new church, and you fit that situation.

Select the most reasonable course of action

You have engineering qualifications and some church leadership experience. Therefore the most reasonable course of action is to start from there.

Having got that far, you should be able to make a confident start on the process of linking up with an agency that is asking for someone like you.

Another word of caution is necessary here. Human reasoning has been affected by sin and our minds can reach wrong conclusions based upon good evidence. So saturate each step of reasoning in prayer.

God is a God of both stability and surprises. He sometimes acts in ways we cannot understand. He takes the most unlikely people and uses them. Gladys Aylward was not considered suitable material for overseas missionary service, but God was working to another agenda. He called her to serve him, she obeyed and touched the lives of thousands. By all means let us use our God-given intelligence to discover the way God is directing us, but never rule out the unexpected. Put that alongside what the Bible is saying to you, what you are discovering in prayer and from your innermost spirit and you will have further reinforcement of the way that God is leading you.

The advice and counsel of friends

Filling in my income tax return is not one of my favourite recreations. But the law requires that I do so, so I do. At first it was a laborious and complicated chore. All that official jargon and the threats about making false statements added to the pressure. Many times I found myself stuck and irritated, confused by the questions and groping in the darkness for answers.

Today it is different. Why the change? No, I haven't taken a special course in Government form answering, nor have I ceased to fill the forms in. I went to a friend for help and advice. He applied his special skills and vast experience in tax returns to my situation. It was a replay of Genesis 1:3—'. . . and there was light!'

As believers we are part of the body of Christ (1 Corinthians 12). We live in relationships and in fellowship with each other. We are to care for, counsel, and build each other up. Other Christians can be a source of direction and advice for us. Find someone you can trust and talk to. You will need to have confidence in their spiritual judgement and maturity. Don't walk in the counsel of the ungodly (Psalm 1:1) because that leads to disaster. Talk to wise spiritual men and women.

Talking helps to clarify our thinking, to get things into perspective. It is also good therapy because it allows us to off-load our fears and release any suppressed anxieties that may be obstructing our understanding of what God is saying to us. Another advantage is that good advisers can point out our personal weaknesses and strengths and this may help us to see the issue from a different perspective. We can be blind to our own deficiencies or unwilling to acknowledge their importance. Once you have been able to say your bit, listen to the counsel given and recognize the voice of God in it even when it is painful to do so. But remember, in the final analysis it is you who will have to make the decisions. Don't try and transfer that responsibility to others.

If you choose to seek the help of someone who is not in pastoral leadership or oversight in your church fellowship, don't neglect to keep your leaders informed about what God is saying and doing in your life. You will need their support and that of the church in any future service you undertake.

Circumstances

When we love God and want to honour him in our lives, we soon realize that things don't just happen. There are no accidents in God's purposes.

It was no accident that Joseph was sold as a slave, was falsely accused of attempted rape and was sent to prison unjustly. He reminded his brothers, 'You intended to harm me, but God intended it for good to accomplish what is now being done, the saving of many lives' (Genesis 50:20). It was not indigestion that kept King Ahasuerus awake one night and caused him to read the account that brought a reward to Mordecai (Esther chapter 6). It was more than voices in his head that took Philip out of a successful mission in Samaria and left him like a hitch-hiker on a major chariot way. God had taken his man with the answers to meet a man with the questions (Acts 8:26-40).

God is not taken by surprise. He is not panicked by any variation in circumstances. He is always in control. He may move behind the circumstances, but he certainly moves all the circumstances he is behind. Therefore our guidance can come through the arrival of an unexpected letter, the words of a surprise visitor or that 'out of the blue' telephone call. Diversions, delays, frustrations, disappointments, these too have their part to play. As Jim Elliot rightly said, 'God pulls strings through circumstances.' God's will may certainly be described as a mystery at times, but it can never be called a muddle. Obviously we should test our circumstantial evidence by the Scriptures and the prayerful counsel of others, and also by that inward Spirit who urges us forward. As these give support to the circumstances of our life we can be assured that we are still moving in the right direction.

To sum up

Having read this far, do not give up now. There has been a lot to absorb and consider, but there is just a bit more to say. Guidance is a very personal thing and the principles outlined here are not to be seen as rules in a rule book which you have got to keep—or be failed, and thrown away as unusable. Nor are they to be looked at as if they were a recipe, where if you omit one ingredient the product will be of an inferior quality.

More accurately, they need to be seen as a route planner. When you are making a journey you know where you want to get to and you know where you are starting from. The map helps you to get from where you are to where you want to go as conveniently as possible. What you have just read is intended to help you make sure that you are on course as you travel the highway of God's will. When the majority of the indicators begin to point in generally the same direction, you can be confident that you are on the right road. However, the essential requirement in all this is our willingness to be, go and do all that the Lord asks of us, even if that involves hardship, singleness, loneliness, obscurity, tears or death. We ought not to try and manipulate our circumstances, our spiritual advisers, our Bible reading, our prayer and thinking to conform to and confirm what we have already chosen to do. God wants willing submissive servants who will allow him to make the choices (1 Samuel 15:22; John 10:27).

It could be that you feel unworthy or unable to be used by God because of past failure, sin or disobedience. If that's how you feel, recognize this important fact; there are no totally negative experiences in our lives. God is the God of salvation, so all things are redeemable. Tell God that you are sorry about your rebellion, sin, fear. Receive his forgiveness and experience the wonder of his second word. 'The word of the Lord came to Jonah a second time' (Jonah 3:1). And the word of the Lord comes a third, fourth, fifth time as well. Do not keep looking back to what you might have been. If you try to walk forward looking backwards you will fall over. Take God at his word and fix your eyes on Jesus by deliberately looking away from other things (Hebrews 12:2). Understand that God loves you, that the blood of Christ has cleansed you, know that the Spirit has filled you and that your heart is towards God and seeking his perfect will. Then you will be able to sing and enter into the truth of the hymn which states, 'All the way my Saviour leads me.' Discover that and delight in it.

Postscript

God speaks to us in various ways. Perhaps you have been conscious of hearing his voice as you have read this book. Your response to him is of crucial importance. Are you willing to do what he tells you—whatever the cost?

Once you have settled on this matter of obedience, the next question to face is 'What next?' We would suggest that you carefully think through these next steps:

(1) Be informed

Become more aware of God's work in his world. Get hold of literature and magazines on mission that will keep you informed and help you pray intelligently. The addresses below will give you a starting point.

(2) Get involved

Mission needs financial support, and to make that happen God wants to touch your pocket as well as your prayer-life. Regular, committed giving to God's work is an important step along the paths of becoming a world Christian. Make your involvement count.

(3) Start where you are

You cannot serve God by running away from your responsibilities. He has placed you where you are and wants you to begin to serve him right there. Service begins at home. In your own church, community, school, college or place of work. Here are opportunities for you to 'get your hands dirty'.

(4) Share with others

God has given leaders in the local church who are there to counsel and advise. If God is calling you to some form of Christian work then you need to share it with them at the earliest opportunity. Be willing to accept their help and direction. If you are in a situation where it is not possible to share with a leader, then seek out a Christian of maturity whom you can trust. It is important that you are praying with Christian friends—because when God calls someone he confirms it through others.

(5) Ask God

Pray. Spend specific times alone with God allowing him to speak into your life. Learn to listen to his voice through Scripture, the wisdom of other Christians, and the various ways in which he speaks. Be patient. God never hurries. You will not miss his best by accident. If your heart is truly set on doing his will, he will guide you.

> Trust the Lord completely; don't ever trust yourself. In everything you do, put God first, and he will direct you and crown your efforts with success (Prov 3:5-6, The Living Bible).

* * *

The following lists are designed to help you gain the information you need to put into action what you believe God is telling you to do. It is not complete or exclusive. You may discover other organizations, not listed, who can help you.

Dirty Hands was co-sponsored by Saltmine Trust, BYFC, OM, YWAM. The last three mentioned all offer short-term and summer-service opportunities.

Useful addresses

British Youth For Christ, Cleobury Place, Cleobury Mortimer, Nr Kidderminster DY14 8JE. Tel. (0299) 270260.

Saltmine Trust, P.O. Box 15, Dudley, West Midlands DY3 2AN. Tel. (0384) 238224.

Operation Mobilisation, Quinta Christian Centre, Weston Rhyn, Oswestry, Shropshire SY10 7LF. Tel. (0691) 773388.

Youth With A Mission, Holmstead Manor, Staplefield Road, Cuckfield, West Sussex RH17 5JF. Tel. (0444) 55934.

General information on evangelical societies and organizations

Evangelical Alliance, Whitefield House, 186 Kennington Park Road, London SE11 4BT. Tel. (01) 582 02288.

Christian Service Centre, 2 Dukes Avenue, Muswell Hill, London N10 2PT. Tel. (01) 444 6326. (This organization seeks to match the needs of Christian organizations and societies to the skills and gifts of Christians who are available to serve in both a short or long term capacity.)

Bible colleges

All Nations Christian College, Easneye, Ware, Herts SG12 8LX. Tel. (0920) 61243.

Assemblies of God Bible College, Mattersey Hall, Mattersey, Doncaster, South Yorks DN10 5HD. Tel. (0777) 817663.

Belfast Bible College, 119 Marlborough Park South, Belfast BT9 6HW. Tel. (0232) 666267.

Bible Training Institute (Non-residential), 731 Great Western Road, Glasgow, Strathclyde G12 8QX. Tel. (041) 334 9849.

Capernwray Bible School, Capernwray Hall, Carnforth, Lancs LA6 1AG. Tel. (0524) 7333908/9.

Cliff College (Methodist), Calver (via Sheffield), Derbys S30 1XG. Tel. (024688) 2321.

Elim Bible College, Grenehurst Park, Dorking, Surrey RH5 5JE. Tel. (0306) 711238.

Emmanuel Bible College, 1 Palm Grove, Birkenhead, Merseyside L43 1TE. Tel. (051) 652 2342/6650.

Lebanon Missionary Bible College, Castle Terrace, Berwick on Tweed, Northumberland TD15 1PA. Tel. (0289) 6190.

London Bible College, Green Lane, Northwood, Middlesex HA6 2UW. Tel. (09274) 2606.

Moorlands Bible College, Sopley, Christchurch, Dorset BH23 7AT. Tel. (0425) 72369.

Oak Hill College (Anglican), Chase Side, Southgate, London N14 4PS. Tel. (01) 449 0467.

Redcliffe Missionary Training College, 66 Grove Park Road, Chiswick, London W4 3QB. Tel. (01) 994 3408.

Spurgeon's College (Baptist), South Norwood Hill, London SE25 6DJ. Tel. (01) 653 0850.

Other organizations

Campus Crusade, 103 Friar Street, Reading, Berks RG1 1EP. Tel. (0734) 589461.

Christians Abroad, 15 Tufton Street, London SW1P 3QQ. Tel. (01) 222 2165.

Christian Nationals, Wangey Road, Chadwell Heath, Essex RM6 4DB. Tel. (01) 597 6100.

Frontier Youth Trust, 130 City Road, London EC1V 2NJ. Tel. (01) 250 1966.

Gospel Literature Outreach (Christian Brethren), GLO Centre, 78 Muir Street, Motherwell ML1 1BN. Tel. (0698) 63483.

Horizons, Glenmoor Road, Llanelli, Dyfed SA15 2LU. Tel. (05542) 50005.

Links International, Norman Barnes, Oasis House, Essex Road, Chadwell Heath, Romford, Essex RM6 4JA. Tel. (01) 590 8556.

Scripture Union, 130 City Road, London EC1V 2NJ. Tel. (01) 250 1966.

TEAR Fund, 100 Church Road, Teddington, Middlesex TW11 8QE. Tel. (01) 977 9144.

The Father Heart of God

by Floyd McClung

What is God like?

Has he got time for twentieth-century men and women?

Does he really care?

In his work with *Youth with a Mission*, Floyd McClung has met many who suffer from deep emotional hurts and fears.

Time and again it has been the discovery of God as Father—perfect and reliable, unlike any human parent—that has brought healing and liberty.

This book is for you...

...if you find it hard to accept God as a loving father, or
...if you know God's love but would like to share his blessing with others more effectively.

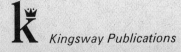

Kingsway Publications

The Cross Behind Bars

*The true story of Noel Proctor—
Prison Chaplain*

by Jenny Cooke

As a boy, Noel Proctor thought that God didn't live
outside the Sunday School classroom. Until something
happened that was to turn his life upside down and
launch him into a totally unexpected career: chaplain to
one of Her Majesty's prisons.

Noel soon discovered that he couldn't convert the
hardened inmates of Britain's prisons singlehanded.
God had to do a deeper work in his life before revival
could come to the nation's 'forgotten people'.

This is the warm and intimate account of how one man
learned to live in the power and will of God, and how his
wife found the courage to fight 'terminal' cancer. Above
all it shows how God's power can be released when his
people put him first in their lives.

Noel Proctor *held chaplaincies
at Wandsworth, Eastchurch and
Dartmoor Prisons before becoming
Senior Chaplain at Strangeways
in Manchester.*

Jenny Cooke *is an adult education
tutor who teaches creative writing.
She is married with three children.*

Kingsway Publications

Is Life So Dear?

by Brother Andrew

Christians have an enemy, and he doesn't always fight fair. The question is: what does it take to win the fierce spiritual battle that is being fought for men's souls?

Brother Andrew is uncompromising in his call for outright commitment to the gospel. With disturbing clarity he shows how the enemy is within our very gates—not in the shape of communism, or Islam, but our own apathy.

Yet his stories of courage and endeavour will inspire us as we see how God equips his servants to take the gospel into enemy strongholds, no matter where we live or where he sends us.

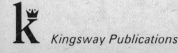

Kingsway Publications